Training to Teach Adults
English

Acknowledgements

We would like to say to thank you to Vera Hutchinson for reading and commenting on a draft of the text and also to all the trainee teachers we have worked with and learnt from.

Training to Teach Adults
English

Irene Schwab with Jane Allemano, David Mallows and Anne McKeown

NIACE The National Voice for Lifelong Learning

Published by the National Institute of Adult Continuing Education
(England and Wales)
21 De Montfort Street
Leicester LE1 7GE

Company registration no. 2603322
Charity registration no. 1002775

NIACE is the National Institute of Adult Continuing Education, the national voice for lifelong
learning. We are an internationally respected development organisation and think-tank,
working on issues central to the economic renewal of the UK, particularly in the political
economy, education and learning, public policy and regeneration fields.

www.niace.org.uk

For details of all our publications, visit http://shop.niace.org.uk

Follow NIACE on Twitter: @NIACEhq
@NIACECymru (Wales)
@NIACEbooks (Publications)

Cataloguing in Publications Data
A CIP record for this title is available from the British Library

978-1-86201-841-9 (Print)
978-1-86201-842-6 (PDF)
978-1-86201-843-3 (ePub)
978-1-86201-844-0 (Kindle)

Produced by Full Stop Communications Ltd, www.fullstopcommunications.co.uk

Cover and text design and typesetting by Patrick Armstrong Book Production Services
Printed in the UK by Charlesworth Press

Contents

Introduction

A typical literacy class in London might consist of 15 or more learners with a diverse range of backgrounds. It is likely that no more than a third of the learners in the class will have been brought up with English as their first language. The profile of an ESOL class will also reveal a multiplicity of backgrounds. Some learners will come from countries where they have had an excellent education, which might have included learning some English; others may never have had any opportunities to learn to read and write their own language, never mind learning English. So as a teacher you will meet language learners in literacy classes and literacy learners in language classes.

Outside London too, there are many cases of people who want to learn to read and write now they are in England. They may not have learned before because their language was never written down (for example, Sylheti, or, until recently, Somali), or because they never had the opportunity to go to school. These are ESOL learners who also need literacy support.

Equally, there are many instances of learners in literacy classes who still have language needs. It is not just those born abroad. Many who were born and brought up in the UK don't regularly use English outside of college; others might have been in the country a long time and picked up English at work or with friends and can speak it fluently, but may have little occasion to read and write it.

Teachers of both literacy and ESOL will frequently come across learners who don't fit neatly into the profile of either a literacy or an ESOL class. Take, for example, Nazir, who was born in the UK and received most of his primary education in London but frequently travelled back to Bangladesh and remained there for his secondary education. He has now returned to London to attend college, but although he still speaks good English, he finds it very difficult to express himself in writing. Or Mariam, who came to England 20 years ago from Somalia. She can carry out everyday tasks in English such as shopping and communicating with her children's school, but she never went to school in Somalia so cannot read or write in Somali or English.

Until 2012, literacy and ESOL teachers trained separately and each developed their own field of expertise. However, as we see from the examples above, learners don't always fit neatly into separate categories of literacy and ESOL. Teachers of ESOL were finding that the traditional methods of language teaching sometimes did not cater for the needs of their learners who needed particular help with literacy. Literacy teachers also found that their training in literacy methods did not provide them with the tools needed to help bilingual learners continue to develop their use of the language. Some teachers found the answer to this dilemma was to complete one set of specialist training programmes and then embark on another so that they had access to both specialisms. Fortunately, since 2012 it has been possible to study literacy and ESOL together in one course, which has not only saved time and money, but it also means that trainee teachers are able to immediately apply their new knowledge of both subjects to support learners in all the different contexts they meet in their teaching practice.

The diversity of the learner body makes the classroom a stimulating and exciting environment but it can also be challenging for the teacher. This book offers support for new teachers or those in training who find themselves in a multilingual ESOL or literacy classroom.

It has been written by a team of literacy and ESOL teacher trainers who have developed a successful PGCE course to train literacy and ESOL teachers. These are dynamic and continually changing subjects and we do not always agree on classroom practice, but we share a belief that there is much to be gained from an understanding of both subjects in order to provide the best possible support for all the learners.

As the majority of literacy and ESOL teachers are women, we have used the pronoun 'she' to refer to teachers in this book. The gender balance for learners is much more even, but to distinguish learners from teachers, we have addressed them as 'he' in the book.

Our aim is to provide a basic introduction to both specialist methodologies. In a book of this size it can only skim the surface but we hope that it will encourage readers to read further and deeper into the topic.

There are eight chapters in the book, covering different aspects of the teacher's role and some of the knowledge that they might need to successfully complete the theoretical and practical elements of a specialist training course. **The learners (Chapter 1)** introduces the reader to the range of learners they might expect to be working with through case studies and the learners' own words. It focuses on the resources learners bring to the learning situation and discusses how teachers can build on their previous experience. It considers the variety of goals that learners might have and explores ways of discussing and negotiating the learning curriculum with them.

Approaches to ESOL and literacy teaching (Chapter 2) explore some basic learning theory and, more importantly, how it can be applied to teaching language and literacy. Generic adult learning theory is related to pedagogy and some specific literacy and language learning techniques and strategies are covered by linking them to relevant theoretical ideas.

The teaching and learning cycle (Chapter 3) builds on on some of the information in the previous chapters. It covers the range of activities that effective teaching depends upon, such as diagnostic assessment (for identifying learner needs), planning lessons which are focused on language and literacy, checking learning and assessing learner progress.

Teaching practice (Chapter 4) focuses on practical teaching. It takes the new teacher through their first steps in the classroom, considering the learning environment and the beginnings of effective classroom management. It explores the different forms of teaching practice (working with individuals and groups, training classes and group teaching practice) and how these might be affected by context. Pointers are given about how to make full use of the learning opportunities offered by teaching practice and how to work effectively with a mentor.

The next two chapters explore the key content of ESOL and literacy classes: developing knowledge of language and skills. **Language knowledge (Chapter 5)** lays the foundations of knowledge about language for the new teacher. It explores what teachers need to know about the language systems of English and offers a framework based on the (English) adult literacy and ESOL national core curricula. This model differentiates between three dimensions of reading and writing: word focus (vocabulary, phonology/phonics and spelling), sentence focus (grammar and punctuation) and text focus (discourse and genre). It also explores the language knowledge needed to teach speaking and listening. **The four skills (Chapter 6)** focuses on how a teacher might work towards helping learners develop their competence in speaking, listening, reading and writing). The chapter explains what techniques are common to the teaching of language and literacy and where methods might differ depending on the language and literacy needs of the learners.

Planning for inclusive practice (Chapter 7) explores the factors a teacher needs to take into account when planning for teaching language and/or literacy. Planning can be the most challenging aspect of teaching for new teachers and this chapter focuses on how to make lessons and courses relevant and interesting for the learners by contextualising the language and literacy learning. It explores ways of building positively on the diversity within the classroom and discusses how a teacher can make their teaching accessible to all learners.

Finally, **Professionalism and continuing professional development (CPD) (Chapter 8)** explores the term 'professional' in relation to the language or literacy teacher. Readers are invited to interrogate the term and consider how the professional standards for teaching in the sector relate to literacy and ESOL teaching. It also looks at ways in which new teachers may continue to develop as reflective practitioners. It invites new teachers to consider what they have learned already and how to address any gaps that they perceive in their knowledge and skills. It explores how they can plan their further development through CPD.

1 | The learners

Irene Schwab

INTRODUCTION

The learners you will meet in a literacy or ESOL class will be as varied as any group of people you might meet in other circumstances. The main thing they will have in common is that they want to improve their use of English – oral or written, or both. Their reasons for joining the class are likely to be varied, as will be their approach to learning. It is up to the teacher to find out what each learner wants from their classes and to try and provide learning opportunities that address these wishes and needs in a way that matches their interests and ways of learning. To do this, they need to know something about the learners.

If you attend a drawing class, the teacher may need to know very little about you in order to help you improve your drawing. However, if you attend a language or literacy class, the teacher will need to know quite a bit more in order to help you improve your skills in using English.

In every learning situation, language is the means of communication, but in ESOL and literacy classes it is also what is being learned; it is both the medium and the message. Language and literacy are closely aligned with individual identity so that in order to help someone communicate better, the teacher needs to know the part that language and literacy (in both English and other languages) currently plays in learners' lives and what their purposes and intentions are in using English.

 **TASK 1.1**

Which of these seven learners might you find in a literacy class and which in an ESOL class?

Kwame

I was born in Ghana and spoke Twi at home. I had primary and secondary education in Ghana in English. I have lived in Sheffield for six years, working as a porter in the NHS, where I mostly speak English. I'd like to improve my education to get better-paid work.

Tomas

I am a migrant worker from Poland. I have an engineering degree from Poland and I studied English as a foreign language at school for five years. I arrived in the UK two years ago and have been working as a labourer on construction sites. I speak Polish at home and with friends. Many of my co-workers are also Polish speakers so I don't have to use much English at work. I want to improve my English in order to develop a career in engineering.

Regis

I was born in the Congo and speak Lingala with my friends and family. My education was very disrupted by the war and I was only able to attend school intermittently, but I learnt to speak French there. I arrived in the UK at the age of 15 and attended secondary school in London for a year. I have a part-time job in a fast food outlet, where I have to use English and I also speak English with my English friends. I don't want to work here forever and I'd like to get some qualifications and possibly go on to higher-level study.

Amina

I am from Somalia. I speak Somali and a little Arabic, although I don't know how to read and write either language. I never went to school in Somalia. I came to London as a refugee five years ago and my daughter was born here.

Jack

I am a dairy farmer in Cumbria. My family has lived in this area for three generations. I only know English, although folks say I have a strong regional accent and use a lot of dialect words. I went to the local school, although I did miss a lot due to having to help out on the farm and left when I was fifteen to work on the farm. Farming today needs much more reading and writing so I need to improve my skills.

Pearl

I was born in St Lucia and my first language was French-Creole. I attended primary school, where I learned English but my parents couldn't afford to send me to secondary school. I came to live in Manchester forty years ago where I married and brought up a family. Although I still use Creole with my family, I use English for work and with my English friends. I've been elected secretary of my tenants' association and would like to improve my English skills.

Irfan

I was born in Pakistan but moved to England with my family when I was five. I can speak English and Urdu. I have dyslexia and a bit of a stammer but I didn't need to go to a special school. I'd like to join a training course in retail but I'm worried that my speaking in English will let me down.

As you can see, adult learners come to classes with a wide variety of experiences and backgrounds. They may come with many skills, some of which might be highly respected within their own communities, for example, in running a successful business or a position of responsibility within their faith community. Others will also have skills and experiences, but these may not be so highly valued either within their communities or by themselves, for example raising children, managing a limited household budget or making music. No one comes to a class as an empty vessel and it is important for the teacher to recognise these skills and experiences as a benefit to the class as a whole and to identify them as a valuable resource to utilise in building additional language and literacy skills.

FACTORS THAT IMPACT ON LEARNING

Learners have different purposes for learning and often need different materials to maintain their interest in learning. In a literacy class, you might find learners similar to these:

> ❱ Melanie has two young children. She wants to read stories to her children and to help them as they begin to learn to read.

> ❱ Abdul wants to go to college to train to be a chef. He needs to improve his English to get on an apprenticeship.

Melanie might be happy to practise reading by using children's books, while this might not be appropriate for Abdul, who may prefer to work with non-fiction texts, especially in his area of interest. Melanie might need to write letters to her children's school or send emails to the council housing department. Abdul, on the other hand, might be interested in writing recipes or drawing up a CV.

A learner's purpose for learning is just one of the factors that the teacher needs to be aware of in order to prepare a relevant learning programme. Others include the following.

> ❱ **Personal and social factors:** These might include factors related to the learner's background, family circumstances, and work and leisure interests.

> ❱ **Linguistic factors:** These might include the languages the learner uses and their facility in each, in terms of the four skills. It is also relevant to know how each of these languages is used in everyday life. For example, a learner born in the UK from a Bangladeshi family might use Sylheti to speak with her parents, Bengali to write to her family back in Bangladesh, English to chat to her friends and workmates and Arabic to read in the mosque.

> ❱ **Cognitive factors:** The impact of brain function on learning is also important. We all learn in different ways and what suits one learner might not be appropriate for another. In addition, learning disabilities (which may or may not have been previously recognised) might have an impact on learning as well as affecting how learners feel about learning.

> ❱ **Educational factors:** Some ESOL learners come to language classes with successful previous learning experiences. They might have a university education or professional qualifications. Others may never have had the opportunity for any education at all. Many will be somewhere in between. Literacy learners, likewise, may never have had the

opportunity to access education, or they may have attended school and been failed in some way by the system at the time. Illness, family responsibilities, disabilities (physical, cognitive or sensory), bullying, truancy, an unmotivating and irrelevant curriculum or just having their needs ignored by the school system may all have prevented them from learning earlier. Some learners say that they could see no point in learning when they were young and it is only later, perhaps when they have families of their own, or need to find a job, that they recognise its relevance to their life.

❯ **Affective factors:** There are many reasons why learners might find it hard to feel positive or motivated in a class. These may relate to previous learning experiences or to current feelings of negativity or alienation. The consequences of a lack of schooling, interrupted education or exam failure are likely to be considerable. Many literacy learners feel alienated from education or may feel that they themselves are failures. They might have been told they were stupid or slow learners. In an ESOL class, recent arrivals in the country might be suffering from trauma and bereavement if they are refugees from war or persecution. Even if they are not, they might be feeling homesick and displaced. These affective factors can impact severely on learning.

Teachers of adult learners often report that the learners are more enthusiastic than teenagers because they have chosen to come to classes. However, as a teacher, you may also be faced with those who are not in a class entirely voluntarily. They may have been sent by the job centre or their employers, they may be offenders in a secure institution, or they might have to study English as part of their vocational course. An awareness of how learners might feel about studying will help a teacher to plan learning programmes that are stimulating and motivating.

 TASK 1.2

Look at these factors and think about ways in which they may affect learning.

1. Whether the learner can read and write in their first language

2. What the learner feels about their previous educational experiences

3. Whether the learner uses English outside the classroom

4. Whether the learner has dyslexia or any other learning difficulty

5. How the learner feels she learns best

6. Whether the learner came to this country from a war zone

7. Whether the learner lives alone or with family or friends

8. What language the learner uses to access the Internet

9. What sorts of things the learner does in his/her leisure time

10. Whether the learner is employed

11. Whether the learner had any education beyond primary level

12. Whether the learner has children

13. What the learner's preferred language is for speaking

14. Whether the learner was bullied at school

Place them under the appropriate heading:

a) Personal and social, b) Linguistic, c) Cognitive, d) Educational, e) Affective

Personal and social factors

❱ **Age**: Often, but not always, younger learners find it easier than older learners to pick up a new language. Younger learners are certainly likely to be more adept at using technology and the majority of them will be accessing websites and texting in their own language or in English, even if their literacy is limited. Younger learners might find it harder to maintain concentration and need shorter, pacier tasks. Older learners might prefer a slower pace with more repetition to aid learning.

❱ **Aspirations:** Learners approach their literacy and ESOL classes with a diverse range of aspirations. They may want practical help, for example in accessing health professionals or contact with their children's school but they may already lead successful and productive lives and need no help at all. They may want to improve their job prospects either by gaining employment, a better job or training for future employment, but they may also be retired or be unable to work for health reasons and have no employment-related needs at all. They may want a general education, having missed out on it earlier in life, or they may be very focused on specific goals. An apprentice plumber with a growing family will have very different aspirations from a retired machinist with grandchildren or a teenage refugee aiming for university.

❱ **Home environment:** The learner's home situation may impact on their learning too. It will certainly affect how much time and space they have for independent study. They may have a computer at home, but they may also have to share it with children or flatmates, which might make access intermittent and difficult. Women, in particular, may have many home responsibilities, which could interfere with their ability to do independent study at home.

Linguistic factors

Some learners may have been in England for many years before seeking help with their English. They may have lived and worked in a community where their own language was sufficient for all their needs. Some women may have stayed at home to raise children and where it was necessary to interact with English speakers, they were supported by English-speaking family members who could interpret for them. Others may have built up an 'interlanguage', a form of English that allows them to communicate successfully with English speakers. An interlanguage is heavily influenced by a learner's own first language and also by generalisations from imperfectly learned rules of English. It is, therefore, not completely accurate English but it is generally perfectly understandable. These learners might be found in a literacy class as well as an ESOL class as they can already communicate in English. However, even though they use oral English confidently in spoken English they might still need language as well as literacy support.

As well as those who are settled in the country, there will also be new arrivals who are in the UK for employment or as refugees or asylum seekers. Their needs in terms of language and literacy will be more immediate. These learners would probably be placed in an ESOL class unless their English was already very strong.

In a literacy class, there will also be those who have English as their first, and maybe only, language. They are likely to use a variety of English that relates to a particular region – either in the four home nations (England, Scotland, Wales, Northern Ireland) or elsewhere in the English-speaking world (such as Caribbean and African countries, or the Republic of Ireland). Their own variety, which might differ in terms of grammar and vocabulary, will have an impact upon their reading and writing in Standard English. Indeed, for some learners whose own variety of spoken English is very different from Standard English, it will be like learning to write in another language.

Languages spoken: It is always useful for the teacher to have some knowledge of what other languages the learner speaks. She will understand their errors much better if she is able to see where these originate from in a home language. Many European languages and some from Asia, in particular the Indian sub-continent, share a common root. These are called Indo-European languages and those who speak one of these languages might be able to draw on its similarities with English. But of course there are also false friends, where words seem to be similar but in fact mean very different things; for example, 'sensible' in French does not mean 'showing good sense' as it does in English, but 'sensitive' or 'nervous'. Likewise, 'embarazada' in Spanish does not translate as 'embarrassed' but in fact means 'pregnant'.

Languages written: If a learner already knows a language that uses the Roman script, this will make it easier for them to learn to write English. Many languages do not use the Roman script and some, for example Arabic, are written from right to left. An Arabic speaker, therefore, will not only need to learn to form a whole new set of letters, but also rethink the direction of their writing. Arabic, like some other languages, also has different punctuation marks or marks that look like those used in English but are used in a different way.

Cognitive factors and other disabilities

Learners with a cognitive disability such as dyslexia might need different teaching approaches. However, adjustments to materials and approaches for dyslexic learners often benefit all learners in the group.

Learners with a physical disability might need adjustments to the environment to make learning accessible; learners with sensory impairments often need amendments to materials and approaches to improve accessibility. The Equality Act 2010 requires that reasonable adjustments must be made to provide accessible learning opportunities.

Mental illness might make it difficult for learners to work in groups and also affects their ability to concentrate and learn. In addition, those who have experienced war or torture in their country might be suffering from shock or trauma.

Most educational institutions will have an equality and diversity policy which will show how the college meets legislation and promotes diversity. Larger educational institutions, such as further education colleges, will also have a team who can support learners with disabilities and advise teachers on best practice.

Educational factors

Some learners coming to an ESOL class will be highly educated and well-qualified in their own country. Doctors, engineers and teachers might have come to this country to seek asylum. They will be used to being in an educational environment and may have excellent study skills. They are likely to have the resources to study independently and may already speak several languages.

At the other extreme, there may be some learners who have little or no previous experience of education either in their own country or in the UK. There are many reasons why this might be the case: war disrupting the educational system; a cultural tradition that does not value the education of girls; illness or disability that prevented school attendance; alienation from school and truancy; or parents who needed their children to care for younger siblings at home or to work to bring money into the family. Many countries still do not have a free educational system and those without the resources to pay miss out on educational opportunities.

In an ESOL class, the teacher is likely to be faced with these extremes and this makes for challenging teaching. In some organisations, learners with little previous education who are not literate in their own language might be found an ESOL/literacy class where they can work on their reading and writing as well as learning the language.

In a literacy class, there are not usually such extremes of educational background. Many literacy learners have had a negative experience of education and as a result might feel alienated from it; that it is 'not for them' or that they are unable to learn effectively. One of the challenges for a literacy teacher is to make education stimulating and accessible for these 'second chance' learners, those who have been failed by the system in their first attempt.

There will be others who have had various levels of disruption in their education, or were maybe just unable to relate to education at the time it was offered. The teacher will need to approach each learner as an individual, listening to what they say about education and drawing on what they already know and can do. People who come to classes to improve their English are adults with a lifetime's experience behind them and it is important to remember that a beginner reader is not a beginner thinker. They may have responsible jobs, families and respected positions within their own communities. Despite difficulties in accessing the spoken and/or written English language, they all have at least one language (and frequently more) that they have already mastered. No one living in Western society will be a stranger to print and they will have had access to many kinds of texts, including those found online. So every learner comes with a wealth of experience that the teacher can draw on.

Affective factors

Country of origin/reason for being in the country: Learners in an ESOL class will tend to be those who have settled in this country. This is unlike an English as a Foreign Language (EFL) class, where most learners are visitors to the country, often here just to improve their English. An ESOL learner may have many reasons for being in the country. They may be refugees and asylum seekers escaping war or oppression in their own country. Alternatively, they may have come here because of a job or be seeking work; they may be accompanying other members of their family or they may be entirely alone. Although it may not have been their choice to leave their homeland, ESOL learners are often highly motivated to learn the language. However, as we saw earlier there may be complex reasons why they might find this difficult and why they might have conflicting feelings about learning English.

Above we can see there is quite a lot of information to acquire and the teacher is not going to find it all out at once. Look back at the learners in Task 1.1. How do you think the teacher has found this information out?

Some of it she will have learned through the enrolment process when a learner applies for a class (initial assessment) or when he joins a class (diagnostic assessment). But most of it is found out by simply talking to each learner. The most crucial element in beginning work is to talk to the learners and listen to what they have to say. They will be able to give you key information about what they know already and what they want to learn; how they use or would like to use the language.

Language and literacy

One of the things a teacher needs to know about the learners is how much language and literacy each already has. It is very unlikely that you will meet learners who have no spoken language at all, unless they have profound learning difficulties. But you may well meet learners in all the other categories.

Speaking and listening

The learner may:

- **have little or no spoken language in any language**. You are very unlikely to meet learners with no spoken language unless they have profound learning difficulties.

- **speak a non-European language**, such as Turkish or Arabic. Speakers of non-Indo-European languages may have very different understandings of grammar and may be used to writing in a different script.

- **speak a European language**, such as French or Spanish. European language speakers may come from the EU and have extensive previous education experience but they may also come from Latin America or Africa where they may have had fewer educational opportunities.

- **speak fluent English**. A learner who speaks fluent English is likely to need either a specialist

English class (to develop their language for particular purposes) or a literacy class (if they need to develop their reading and writing in English).

Reading and writing

The learner may:

> **have little or no literacy in any language**. These learners will need specialist support in either a literacy or an ESOL class to develop their reading and writing skills.

> **have literacy in a language that does not use the Roman script**, such as Bengali or Urdu. If a learner does not yet know the Roman script, they will need extra support in learning to read and write in English.

> **have literacy in a language that uses the Roman script**. If a learner already uses the Roman script, acquiring literacy in English is likely to be easier than if they also have to learn the script.

> **have literacy in English**. These learners will probably be in a literacy class. They may need to develop their literacy for specific purposes, such as for academic study, for work, or training for work.

 TASK 1.3

How might the following learners from Task 1.1 (p. 4) fit the profile above?

Tomas

Amina

What might be the challenge for a teacher in teaching both Amina and Tomas in the same class?

Adult learners are not like children; they bring considerable experience of life and practical and creative resources to the learning situation. They support their families, raise children, maintain jobs and may well be engaged in many aspects of their own cultural and social groups. These experiences are sometimes called 'funds of knowledge'. Funds of knowledge are valuable cultural and educational resources, but they are not always recognised or valued by educational institutions. Effective teachers will draw on these funds of knowledge to enhance their teaching. There are two significant teaching approaches language and literacy teachers can use to build on these funds of knowledge. They are particularly valuable for work with beginner learners who might find reading, writing and/or speaking English difficult.

The *reflect ESOL* approach uses visual learning materials related to learners' own immediate experiences and links the development of language skills to relevant issues in learners' lives. It enables participants to bring their existing knowledge, skills and creativity into the learning process and to express their own opinions in ways that do not rely on facility with the English language.

The *language experience* approach is used in both literacy and ESOL teaching, although there are slight differences in technique. The learner and teacher talk together and record what the learner says. The teacher writes it down and helps the learner read back their own words, using these words as a reading text that has real meaning for the learner and draws on their own language patterns and vocabulary.

Both these approaches can also be used as a way to develop other skills such as speaking or writing.

A social practice approach to literacy involves taking account of the learners' lives and what they do or want to do with the language. We call what people do with literacy their literacy *practices*. These can be complex and varied. For example, as individuals they might keep a diary or make up stories for their children; they might surf the net, make lists and leave notes. As members of society some learners might contribute to an online forum; they might write to friends and relatives back home; they might belong to a club, society or faith community; they might be members of their children's school PTA or their union at work. They probably text their friends and access Facebook. These uses of literacy are significant and relevant for the teacher who can draw on them for ideas, authentic and motivating materials and ways of engaging each learner.

FURTHER READING

Appleby, Y. and Barton, D. (2008) *Responding to People's Lives*. Leicester: NIACE.

Cooke, M. and Simpson, J. (2008) 'A world of difference: Being an adult ESOL learner', in id., *ESOL: A Critical Guide*. Oxford: Oxford University Press.

Fowler, E. and Mace, J. (2005) *Outside the Classroom: Researching Literacy with Adult Learners*. Leicester: NIACE.

2 Approaches to literacy and language teaching

Irene Schwab

INTRODUCTION

This chapter explores the pedagogy of literacy and language teaching. Even though literacy and ESOL learners often overlap and have similar needs, literacy and ESOL teaching draw on very different pedagogical approaches. ESOL is part of the international world of English language teaching and has benefited from a great deal of research and development. While we still may not know exactly how people learn to speak a second language, there are many methods that have been tried and tested and can be adapted for use with ESOL learners. Adult literacy, on the other hand, has been under-researched and under-developed and it is only now that a pedagogy is being established.

On an initial teacher education course, you will come across many different approaches to teaching. As you become more experienced in teaching, you will incorporate some of these into your practice; some will work only in certain contexts and with certain groups. It is important to develop a way of reflecting on your practice so that you are able to examine different techniques and critique them in terms of their effectiveness for the particular group of learners you are working with.

Because they are derived from different traditions, approaches to literacy and ESOL teaching have developed in different ways but the aim is always to provide the best possible learning opportunities for all learners. In the following section we look at some approaches used in teaching ESOL and literacy separately. However, in practice, and with some adaptations, most of these can be used with both groups of learners. There may be a different emphasis in the classroom, with ESOL groups spending as much, or more, time on speaking and listening activities as on reading and writing (especially for beginners), whereas literacy groups tend to focus on reading and writing, although speaking and listening will be used to generate and discuss ideas, and support their understanding of written texts.

It is important for a teacher to be aware of the learners' knowledge of language in deciding which techniques are appropriate. Issues around the use of language can occur in both ESOL and literacy classes and the language learning techniques outlined below can be utilised. Likewise, literacy needs can also occur in both and then literacy approaches can be used, although the teacher of an ESOL class will always need to bear in mind the need to ensure that the meaning of words is known and grammatical structures are understood in order to interpret written language.

Pedagogy is defined by the *Oxford English Dictionary* as 'the theory or principles of education and a method of teaching based on such a theory.' We can see from this that one definition covers two different views: a practical view (what a teacher does) and a theoretical view (what a teacher believes). In practice, these may not be quite so divergent because what a teacher does depends very much on what she believes.

Figure 2.1 below shows how our expectations of teaching and learning are influenced by our own experiences of education and how well they worked for us; they may depend on what we think education is and what it is for; how we believe people learn and what we think they should be learning. In other words, our understandings about pedagogy are formed by our own beliefs and experiences of the educational process, which are set within the context of our own political, social and cultural background and view of the world.

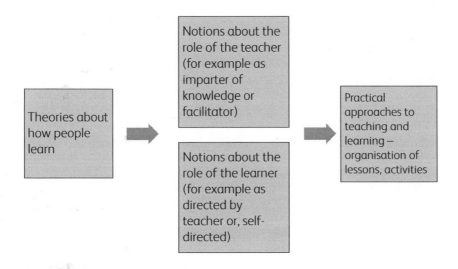

Figure 2.1. The relationship between theory and practice

The word *pedagogy* derives from a Greek term meaning, literally, 'to lead or tend the child'. However, it is common to talk about pedagogy for both adults and children, despite the fact that adults and children learn in different ways. Malcolm Knowles (Knowles, Holton and Swanson, 2011), coined the term *andragogy* to distinguish adult learning processes from those of children. He argued that adults are different from children in five key ways:

> ❯ They are self-directed (independent learners)

> ❯ They have a range of experiences that can be used as a resource for their learning

> ❯ They need learning to be relevant to their own situation

> ❯ They need learning to be usable immediately

> ❯ Their motivation to learn may be *intrinsic* (learning for its own sake, because it is personally fulfilling or enjoyable, for example) rather than *extrinsic* (the desire to learn something in order to be rewarded in some way, for example to pass an exam or to obtain a job)

These principles of andragogy may not, of course, be true for all learners in all situations. For example, some learners enjoy abstract knowledge for its own sake and some may lack intrinsic motivation and need the challenge of certification to motivate them. But in general, these factors make working with adults, even young adults, very different from working with children.

Theories about how adults learn can be divided into those that take a cognitive view of learning and those that take a social view. A cognitive (or psychological) view of learning sees it as a process that occurs in an individual's brain. A social view of learning, on the other hand, perceives it as a social process – occurring within a social and cultural context. These are often set in opposition to each other but in practice both should play a part in your approach to teaching, even if you feel more strongly about one than the other.

 TASK 2.1

Here are some statements about learning. Which do you think fit with a cognitive view of the learning process and which with a social view?

❯ Learners learn best in groups

❯ People need to do a variety activities in different ways to help them learn

❯ Learners learn best on their own

❯ People need lots of repetition to help them learn

❯ Education is where learners follow their own routes to learning

❯ Materials should be carefully controlled so that the learners are not faced with anything beyond their level

❯ Education is where the teacher shares what she knows with her learners

❯ Materials should be those encountered in real life (realia)

COGNITIVE THEORIES OF LEARNING

There have been a number of different attempts to describe cognitive or psychological processes. Here we look at three: behaviourism, humanism and constructivism.

Behaviourism

Behaviourism, which derives from the work of Skinner (1974), suggests that learning is about conditioning. Behaviourists believe in breaking down complex learning tasks into small steps and then moving forward with small repetitive steps, with the teacher offering positive reinforcement of each correct stage. Positive reinforcement might be in the form of good marks, ticks in the margin or oral praise: 'Well done, you got that right'.

While it can be criticised for being a somewhat mechanical approach, breaking down learning into small steps or chunks and staging them, and giving praise and encouragement to learners, are widely acceptable approaches. Below are a couple of examples of teaching approaches based on behaviourism.

> **Drilling**, used extensively in ESOL teaching, is the oral repetition of words, phrases or sentences in order to practise certain aspects of language for example, the pronunciation of words or the response to statements or questions. Drilling can be individual or choral.

> **Look, say, cover, write, check** is a strategy for learning spellings, which uses visual (look), aural (say) and kinaesthetic (cover, write) techniques. By checking and then repeating the procedure, the learner uses repetition and gives himself positive reinforcement when he gets it right.

Humanism

Humanistic psychology approaches learning with an emphasis on process rather than product. The learner's feelings are understood to be as important as their cognitive abilities. The teacher is seen as facilitator, more than provider, of learning and the emphasis is on learner-centred pedagogy. Learning theorists have suggested ways in which the teacher could take account of these views, for example Krashen (1985) argued for 'the lowering of the affective filter', i.e. making the learner feel relaxed and comfortable in order to learn better. Maslow (1970) also argued for a comfortable environment and meeting learners' physical and emotional needs to help them achieve their ultimate aims. Examples of teaching approaches based on humanism include the following:

> **Communicative approaches** to ESOL learning. These involve using the language in authentic and meaningful ways rather than learning rules, with activities such as role play and simulation involving the learner in using language for real purposes.

> **Reading circles** might be used in literacy classes, where learners choose their own books to read and support each other in reading them. The teacher plays a minimal role, facilitating only where necessary.

Constructivism (and social constructivism)

Constructivists argue that learners make sense of new knowledge by integrating it into what they already know. Social constructivism or activity theory has developed from the work of Vygotsky (Vygotsky and Kozulin, 2012), who believed that learning is an interactive process and that sharing with others can help us build new knowledge. One implication of this is the idea that we learn best by being given work that is just beyond the level of our current knowledge, what Vygotsky called 'the zone of proximal development' (ZPD). In this state, we can be helped to move forward by working with more knowledgeable others or through the use of appropriate materials through which we are assisted to do an activity that would be too difficult without support. The process of providing this supportive framework is called 'scaffolding'. Examples of teaching approaches based on social constructivism include the following.

❭ **Writing frames** can help learners attempt a writing task that might be difficult for them by providing the basis of a structure. The frame might contain prompts or the beginnings of sentences for the learners to complete with their own writing, for example drafting a three paragraph complaint letter:

> I am writing to complain about................................
>
> When I got it home, ...
>
> I am not happy with this and I would like you to...................................

❭ **Pre-reading activities** will help learners create more meaning from what they read. They involve sharing what people already know about a subject and also filling in some of the gaps in order to make the topic more familiar and accessible. For example, before reading a newspaper article you might start by:

- eliciting from each learner what they already know about it (this is called activating the learners' schema);

- writing up these contributions on the board in the form of a diagram to show how these ideas fit together;

- looking at a map or website together to fill in possible gaps in knowledge that will contextualise the reading; and

- going over any key vocabulary that will be found in the text to be read, discussing what they might expect to find in the article (prediction), or devising questions (question generation) that they would like answered by reading the text.

SOCIAL THEORIES OF LEARNING

These depend on a view of learning as dependent on our relations with others, rather than as an internal and individual process.

Social practice theory

This approach sees learning as situated social practice. This means that learning never takes place in isolation, but always within a social, cultural, historical and political context. Social theories have been particularly influential in forming our view of literacy as multifaceted. In fact, we often refer to *literacies* in the plural, in recognition that forms of literacy differ according to where and how they are used. Taking a social view of literacy involves thinking about *literacy events* – occasions where written texts are used in people's lives; and *literacy practices* – more general behaviour around written texts (incorporating literacy events, but with an emphasis on what we do with texts on a more regular basis). For example, when I turn to my notebook in order to look up my mother's recipe for cheesecake, I am taking part in a *literacy event*, but the practice of cooking by the use of written recipes (as opposed to cooking by trial and error or from memory) is a *literacy practice* that is used in some cultures but not others.

If we see literacy (or literacies) as situated within their social context, we notice that written texts themselves are also a product of the social context in which they are written, produced and distributed. We all recognise that advertisements are designed to persuade us to buy or do something, but information leaflets, text books, instruction manuals, newspaper articles and even some novels and children's books may also contain greater or lesser elements of persuasion which may be a good deal more subtle than in an advertisement. The ability to recognise where and how such techniques are used and to be able to control language to employ them for one's own ends is called *critical literacy*. Critical literacy involves analysing the purpose and intended audience of texts and the impact this has on the message they offer. A social view of learning would regard a critical approach as a fundamental aspect of learning.

Another feature of social practice theory is the idea of learning being 'situated' or seen within its context. Language and literacy is not something that we can learn in isolation from the rest of our lives; it is always used for a purpose within a particular situation. Fluent users of the language adapt how they use literacy to fit the situation and achieve their purposes. This is called 'contextualisation' and it follows that if we use language within a context, we should also *learn* it within a context. A social view of learning avoids decontextualised learning (for example, lists of disconnected spellings or disembodied grammar rules) and always links the learning to its social context. Examples of teaching approaches based on social practice theory include the following.

❯ **Situated learning** is learning 'by doing', so that what is learned is in context and applied immediately. One type of situated leaning is embedded language and literacy learning in which language and literacy are studied through another subject. For example, if a learner is training to work in childcare, she might learn reading through looking at articles or books on child development, writing through reports or observations of small children, and speaking and listening through discussions and presentations about children and their care. Vocabulary learned would also relate to the childcare context.

❯ **Collaborative reading/writing approaches**. Reading circles provide an example of collaborative reading. Writing can also be a collaborative act with learners working in pairs or small groups to draft a text together. Alternatively, they could work on composing a text jointly by each working on separate components, or in sequence, with one doing the first draft and another helping with the revision and editing process.

Transformative learning

This is not so much a way of learning as a principle which underpins a view of learning. It derives from the work of Freire (1972), who believed that the role of education is to promote change and transform the lives of those who partake in it. Freire developed an approach to the teaching of literacy to adults in Brazil, using images of powerful concepts to promote discussion of these concepts at the same time as learning of the writing of relevant vocabulary. Examples of teaching approaches based on transformative learning include the following.

❯ The **reflect ESOL approach** (see Chapter 2) is rooted in Freirian ideals of social change and uses participatory methodologies which place learners at the centre of the learning process, with the teacher becoming a facilitator enabling and sharing the learning process rather than directing it.

❭ The **learner writing and publishing movement**, which encourages learners to develop their own authorial voice and share their ideas and opinions through publication of their work, is an example of transformative learning in a literacy context. Formerly this was predominantly through books and magazines, but more recently through blogging and websites. (See, for example, the NRDC's Voices on the Page project: www.nrdc.org.uk/voicesonthepage.asp).

LANGUAGE AND LITERACY FRAMEWORKS

The Core Curriculum framework

As part of the Skills for Life strategy, the government brought in a set of standards for adult literacy and numeracy. The literacy standards formed the basis of a core curriculum for both literacy and ESOL outlining the skills and knowledge needed in three areas:

❭ **Speaking and listening**: Speak to communicate, listen and respond and engage in discussion

❭ **Reading**: Read and understand and obtain information

❭ **Writing**: Write to communicate

The curriculum operates at three levels of the Qualifications and Credit Framework: Entry Level, Level 1 and Level 2. Entry Level is further divided into three sub-levels (Entry 1, Entry 2 and Entry 3). The curriculum covers work with learners who are just beginning to speak and understand English or to read and write it (Entry 1) as well as those who might be ready for the lower levels of a GCSE qualification (Level 2).

The curriculum framework further focuses on three different dimensions in the processes of reading and writing:

❭ **Text** focus (the overall meaning of the text as whole)

❭ **Sentence** focus (sentence structure including grammar and punctuation)

❭ **Word** focus (vocabulary, spelling and word structure of individual words)

The curriculum framework states that teachers should draw simultaneously on all three dimensions in their work at all levels and lays out what is involved in learning each skill and sub-skill with helpful examples.

Since 2010, the literacy Skills for Life qualifications have been replaced by Functional Skills and other qualifications, which can be taken alone or embedded in other vocational and academic routes. The Functional Skills subject criteria for English (encompassing both literacy and ESOL at the same levels as Skills for Life) have components that are equivalent to the core curriculum:

❭ Speaking, listening and communication

❭ Reading

❭ Writing

However, they are expressed more succinctly in terms of sub-skills to be achieved, which means that teachers have less to cover in order to prepare for examinations, even though, in fact, the skills needed to learn to speak, understand, read and write English remain the same. They have also lost the Text, Sentence, Word framework.

Both the Skills for Life Core Curricula and the Functional Skills subject criteria outline the skills and sub-skills to be learned but do not specify what might be the most helpful way to learn them or how a teacher should approach teaching them effectively. They are 'context-free' which means that it is up to the teacher to find the best way of providing context and content to suit the learners' own interests and priorities.

Language, form and function

The *function* of a language item is its communicative purpose. For example, the language of asking for information might involve several different *forms* (constructions) depending on the situation, such as:

> 'Could you possibly tell me...?' (polite request)

> 'Do you know...?' (informal request)

> 'I'm calling to find out...'(telephone request only)

The form of the language will change according to its function. On the other hand, a particular form might have several different functions, for example:

> Can I turn right here? (asking for information)

> Can I have a lift? (asking a favour)

> Can I smoke here? (asking permission)

As you can see, the relationship between form and function in real-life communication can be complex. ESOL teaching often focuses on functions because by mastering these, learners are able to do everyday things with language like give advice, make requests, apologise and agree or disagree, giving them realistic choices about which form of language they choose to use in any particular context.

APPROACHES TO TEACHING AND LEARNING: LANGUAGE

Teachers often find that having a framework for designing and planning lessons is useful as it ensures that all the elements of a good lesson are present. In the past, language teaching focused on vocabulary and grammar with a lot of input on how the language was structured. However, although this provided plenty of controlled practice, it did not necessarily help learners to use the language in ways that were natural and unscripted.

This method has now largely been replaced by more communicative approaches in which the emphasis is on realistic communication in a variety of contexts and for a variety of communicative purposes. It takes the learners' real uses of the language as a starting point and focuses on expressing authentic content as a means to accuracy of form.

There are a number of ways in which this can be achieved but some sort of explicit language study, controlled practice and free use of the language are likely to play a part, though not in any particular order. There are a number of frameworks in existence, mostly known by a set of initials. We will look at two examples below.

PPP (Presentation, Practice, Production)

Here, a language item is selected by the teacher and presented to the learners in an oral or written context. This is followed by some controlled practice through which learners are able to practise using the chunk of language that is being taught in a manner that is strictly controlled by the teacher, perhaps by drilling (repetition chorally or individually of what the teacher says) or responding to the teacher's cues ('Do you like going to the cinema?' 'Yes, I do'; 'Do you like watching TV?' 'No I prefer going clubbing'). The final stage of PPP is production, where learners use the new language they have learned in ways of their own; this might occur through role plays, discussions or writing activities. PPP is widely used in language teaching. It has been criticised for being overly teacher-centred and for assuming that learning takes place in set ways for all learners, but it can be a good framework for trainees to begin with until they gain more confidence.

ARC (Authentic use; Restricted use and Clarification and focus)

Such concerns led Scrivener (2011) to a less prescriptive form of lesson design. The model he proposes contains largely the same elements as PPP but is more flexible in that the order of the elements of a lesson can be varied. Scrivener maintains that this is a descriptive rather than prescriptive model of a lesson, meaning that it gives a framework for the planning of a lesson rather than specifying what a lesson should look like. A lesson might contain any or all of the ARC components in any order. Naturally this gives more freedom to the teacher, but for new teachers it doesn't offer the same structured approach to lesson design as PPP.

Within these overall designs for lessons, there are a number of methods that are widely used in language teaching, all of which have some merits. It is impossible to cover all methods in a book of this size, so we will concentrate on a couple of key aspects of communicative language teaching.

Inductive learning

In this approach to language learning, learners are given examples of a language structure and they then work out the underlying rules for themselves. This contrasts with the *deductive* approach in which learners are given the rules and then practise applying them. For example, teaching negative forms through a deductive approach might involve the teacher explaining the rules of negation and giving the learners some sentences for controlled practice, orally and in writing. On the other hand, a teacher using an *inductive* approach might show the learners a set of sentences, both positive and negative, like those below. They might be written on cards so that they can be moved around:

❱ I go to work every day

❱ I don't go to work on Saturdays

❱ I go to work five days a week

❱ I go to work on the bus

❱ I don't go to work on the train

❱ I don't go to work when I am sick

The learners would be put into small groups to discuss the sentences and work out the rule for themselves.

Task-based learning

This approach starts from the idea that we all need to use language to carry out particular tasks and that these can be replicated in the classroom. Instead of focusing on language structures, learners use the language to solve a problem or perform a task. The focus is on meaning rather than the language, with the learning of language implicit in the problem solving activity. By its very nature, there are no rights and wrongs in this activity – the important thing is to use language to complete the task. There might be three stages in task-based learning. For example, if the task is to plan a summer outing for the group:

❱ **Pre-task** (teacher-led): The teacher organises the learners into groups; introduces the topic, provides information that might be needed (such as brochures, timetables or access to computers for websites) and maybe highlights some key vocabulary.

❱ **Task cycle** (learner-led): The learners plan and organise how they will do the task; they might assign tasks to individuals or pairs or they might carry out the whole task as a group. The task might be confined to one session or it may be spread over several. When the task is completed (a decision has been agreed), the learners report back either verbally or in writing.

❱ **Language focus** (teacher-led): The final phase is to discuss any language features that arose during the task. These might be at text, sentence or word level and might be instigated by either the teacher or the learners. The teacher might follow up such a discussion with more practice in whatever issues have been raised.

Task-based learning is widely used in language learning, as it focuses on authentic and practical uses of speaking and listening, but it can also be used as a literacy approach, especially in a task like the one described above. In literacy you might hear it described as project-based work.

 ## TASK 2.2

Think about the example of task-based learning above in relation to the ARC approach. Which element of the process might be seen as authentic use of the language (A)? Which might be seen as restricted use (R) and which might be seen as clarification and focus (C)?

APPROACHES TO TEACHING AND LEARNING: LITERACY

Skills and practices

Unlike ESOL, which has several tried and tested methods for teaching, the pedagogy of adult literacy is still being developed. How you choose to teach might well depend on how you view literacy.

> **Skills**: Those who view literacy as a set of skills that people need in order to function in today's society are likely to see a deficit in those who do not possess them. Their aim in the pedagogy is to pass on those skills to the individuals who need them.

> **Social practices:** Those who see literacy as a cultural and social practice, on the other hand, look at the ways people already engage with written texts in their everyday lives and build on what people do and want to do with literacy.

Although sometimes seen as competing pedagogies, it is often useful to draw on an understanding of literacy as both a skill and a social practice. If we look at this profile of a learner we can begin to see the difference between the two approaches.

> **Ron** is 25 years old. He is married with a four-year-old son and lives in a flat in London. He has a job stacking shelves in a local supermarket, where he works shifts. He is attending classes so that he can get a better job with more prospects and also so that he can help his son when he starts learning to read. He can drive. He is interested in football, supporting his team, and is also a member of an astronomy society, which he attends monthly with his telescope.
>
> He reads the labels on the items he handles in the supermarket. He picks up a *Metro* newspaper most mornings so he can share stories with his workmates in the break, but he doesn't find it easy to follow the articles. He tries to work out words but often gets stuck after the first letter. He generally turns to the sport pages first and these are easier for him as he already knows what happened in the previous evening's football matches.
>
> Ron writes very little. He occasionally sends short emails to his sister and texts his friends. He doesn't need to use punctuation to make himself understood. He realises that to get a better job, he will have to improve his writing.
>
> He has been placed in a literacy class where he is working towards an Entry Level 2 Functional Skills qualification.

A skills approach might start with what Ron needs to learn. This will have been determined by his diagnostic assessment. Taking the Entry Level 2 elements of the core curriculum as a guide he might begin with work on:

> phonics (learning the relationship of the sounds within words (*phonemes*) to the symbols (*graphemes*)

> reading short narrative and instructional texts

> writing short texts, using compound sentences and basic punctuation

The emphasis would be to learn skills that are transferable to any situation. He would progress, learning each skill sequentially, building up and using the new skills. The texts used would be those that best exemplify the new skills and knowledge he needs to develop.

A social practices approach might start with what Ron already does with texts:

❭ Reading product labels, articles on football or astronomy, and notices that he might be exposed to at work

❭ Writing stories to read to his son

The emphasis would be on building on what he already knows and does, and on reading and writing for particular contexts. The texts used would be authentic ones taken from newspapers, Internet or employment sources.

The Text, Sentence and Word approach

As we saw above, the core curriculum divides literacy into separate components:

❭ Text focus (the overall meaning of the text as whole)

❭ Sentence focus (sentence structure including grammar and punctuation)

❭ Word focus (vocabulary, spelling and word structure of individual words)

The curriculum argues for an integrated approach, in which all four skills are developed simultaneously and text, sentence and word focus activities are incorporated into planning at all levels. However, at Entry Level the curriculum focuses more at word level, moving towards a more text focus at Levels 1 and 2. This does not necessarily mean that a teacher needs to concentrate on word-level activities at Entry Level, just that these are more carefully defined in the curriculum.

For example, an Entry 3 literacy lesson on healthy eating might consist of the following.

❭ An oral warming-up activity to activate the learners' schema about the topic. This could be a discussion, a quiz or game to share what they know already (speaking and listening/word focus).

❭ Introduction to the reading text, predicting what it might include and what questions it might answer; introduction to any unfamiliar words that might cause problems reading the text (pre-reading activity/text, word focus).

❭ Reading a short leaflet, newspaper article or website giving information about healthy eating – individually or collaboratively (reading activity/text, sentence focus).

❭ Further discussion about what has been read, incorporating learners' own impressions and opinions, checking understanding of the whole text (the gist) and individual sections and words in the text, including any implicit meanings as well as explicit ones (post-reading activity/text, sentence and word focus).

❭ Preparation for writing, involving the teacher modelling the language, structure and layout features of the text type to be reproduced (pre-writing activity/text, sentence and word focus)

❭ Individual or collaborative writing activity (writing activity/text, sentence focus)

❭ Further work on the written text, involving revising, editing and proofreading, maybe to be completed after the session (writing activity/text, sentence and word focus)

In this outline of a session, the main focus is on text level activities, but sentence-level and word-level work is incorporated into both the reading and writing tasks as indicated above. Additionally, further work on any of the elements might occur, if learners raise questions or if it seems apposite to include it. The following session might focus on a different element; for example, it might begin by focusing on vocabulary or spellings arising from the writing.

The genre approach

This approach is based on the idea that texts are produced in conventional ways; they are recognisable because writers follow a set pattern in their construction in terms of structure (how they are built up), layout (how they look on the page or screen) and the language that is used.

It can help reading when the reader can recognise the genre that is being used and knows what to expect. Being able to predict what is likely to be in a text makes it easier to then read it. Likewise for writing, understanding what is expected makes it easier to reproduce a particular type of text. The teacher can model how these texts are constructed and learners can practise analysing models and trying them out for themselves.

 TASK 2.3

Look at the recipe below. What features can you spot that show this is a typical example of the genre? Think about the structure, the layout and the language of a typical recipe.

Leek and potato soup
Ingredients
1 tbsp olive oil
1 onion
250g potatoes
2 medium-sized sliced leeks
1.5 litres vegetable stock
150ml double cream
Salt and pepper

Method
1. Peel and chop the potatoes into 2-3cm cubes. Slice the leeks.
2. Heat the oil in a large pan on a medium heat.
3. Add the potatoes, leeks and onions and cook for about 4 minutes until they begin to soften.
4. Add the vegetable stock to the pan and bring to the boil.
5. Add the salt and pepper to taste, then simmer until the vegetables are soft.
6. Take off the heat and blend until smooth.
7. Stir in the cream, heat the soup and serve with crusty bread and butter
Makes 4-6 portions

A phonic approach

Language is like a code. Understanding the relationship of spoken to written language and how sounds are represented by letters can be a crucial step for developing literacy. By cracking the code, learners are able to build up a strategy for approaching new words and new texts.

The main code that is important here is the link between the letters (*graphemes*) and the sounds (*phonemes*). By learning the letter–sound correspondences that are regular or, at least, the range of regular probabilities, the learner has a tool kit to decode unfamiliar words. Although English famously has many words that do not correspond logically, there are many cases where the links are regular and predictable. Where they are not entirely regular, they are still predictable as there is only a limited range of possibilities. For example, it is most likely that wherever the phoneme /f/ comes in a word, it will be made by the letter *f* (*fork, friend* and *brief*). The sound can also be made by the digraph ph (*photograph, graphics*); and, at the end of a word, by *fe, ff* or *gh* (*safe, gruff, rough*). So when considering the spelling of a word with the sound of /f/ one's best bet would be to try *f* first. On the other hand, the grapheme *f* can make two sounds: /f/ (*fly*) or /v/ (*of*).

It is not a foolproof method; speakers of languages with more regular sound–symbol relationships than English may have difficulty with a phonic approach. Also, learners can often find it difficult to hear the different sounds in words, especially when they use a variety of English that is different from the teacher's. For example, in some varieties of English the words *Mary, marry* and *merry* might be homophones, whereas in other varieties they sound distinct; likewise, *ant* and *aunt* or *due* and *do*.

Some people find differentiating between different sounds very difficult, especially vowel sounds. For these people, decoding aurally may not be the best option for all words. A visual approach whereby one learns the whole word by shape and size can be an option. It is quicker and easier to learn whole words than to have to decode each one individually. A mere twenty-five words make up one third of everything we read; one hundred words are one half. It makes sense to be able to recognise these words quickly and easily, especially as there are also often irregular spellings which can be hard to decode. Using flash cards on their own or in games (like snap, pelmanism or word bingo) can help learners to look carefully at words and remember their shape and form.

Punctuation is another code that we use, as are numbers, emoticons and other abbreviations used in everyday communication.

Critical literacy

A writer always writes for a purpose and with a particular audience in mind. They then design the text to fulfil their purpose and address their intended audience. Sometimes this objective is clear to the reader; sometimes less so. We can analyse any text for meanings over and above the obvious ones. This is called *critical reading* or reading between the lines, in which both explicit and implicit meanings are explored.

Texts are never neutral. Each is produced by a writer who sits within a particular social and cultural context. This person has a reason for writing something and an audience in mind. The teacher can assist the learner in analysing a text to determine what these might be. Who is the text aimed at? You? How do you know? If it isn't you, why might you have been excluded? What techniques and language does the writer use to achieve their object?

Each summer, Transport for London offers advice to the travelling public on how to keep comfortable on the London Underground in the heat. Their 'Stay Cool' campaign has included a poster described in this extract from their press release:

Tube and bus plans to help Stay Cool this summer

07 June 2006

Poster campaign

New style 'Stay Cool' posters will be displayed at all stations bearing the following advice.

Here are a few tips for keeping comfortable in hot weather:

- **Carry water with you**
- **Don't board a train if you feel unwell**
- **If you feel unwell please get off at the next stop and seek help from our staff; and**
- **Avoid pulling the passenger alarm between stations**

Reproduced with permission from https://www.tfl.gov.uk/info-for/media/press-releases/2006/june/tube-and-bus-plans-to-help-stay-cool-this-summer

The poster referred to here was displayed in stations for several years and was, for the travelling public, perhaps the most conspicuous element of the campaign. The wording on the poster, as detailed above, appears to be straightforward. The intended audience was underground train passengers. It is part of the genre of health and safety posters. However, as critical readers we might query if this poster is purely about helping passengers stay safe and healthy or might there be further underlying meanings to discover?

We might choose to analyse this text using the text sentence and word framework. On a word level, we might look at the words that have been used, for example why the pronouns you and our have been chosen and what the effect might have been if different pronouns had been used.

We could also, at sentence level, explore the grammar choices that have been made. Sentences giving instructions usually begin with an imperative verb. Three of these do (one is negative); the fourth doesn't. Why do you think this is? What is the effect? Does it sound more or less important than the others?

Additionally, you might begin to ask bigger questions about the text as a whole. What degree of obligation do these instructions demand? Is it the same for all four 'tips'? Which ask for most compliance? How can you tell? And indeed, interrogating the text like this might take you beyond what is written here towards questions like: According to these instructions, who is responsible for your comfort on the tube? Do you agree with this?

Detailed analysis of how a text is constructed to achieve the author's objective will help learners both to understand more deeply what they read and to make more effective language choices in order to achieve their own intentions.

 TASK 2.4

Look at the headline below from a daily newspaper. What features of the text show the paper's attitude?

Now 78 gypsies ordered to leave illegal camp claim their CHILDREN's 'human rights' mean they should stay put (and you'll foot the £200,000 bill)

Source: http://www.dailymail.co.uk/news/article-2533143/Now-78-gypsies-ordered-leave-illegal-camp-claim-CHILDRENs-human-rights-mean-stay-youll-foot-200-000-bill.html#ixzz2pLprApxr

CONCLUSIONS

In this chapter we have outlined some common approaches used in ESOL and literacy teaching. Although they arise from different traditions, nearly all are suitable for both literacy and ESOL teaching. Teachers will draw on both pedagogies to provide the best possible learning opportunities for their groups, choosing the most appropriate approach for the learners present. This will involve the use of techniques that support the learning of both language and literacy, but these might be focused differently depending on the learners' needs. For example, speaking will be a feature of both literacy and ESOL classrooms, but in an ESOL context, learners are learning to speak English and, at times, teachers will need to correct their speech so that they learn to reproduce the language accurately. An ESOL teacher might employ drilling to help learners focus on the pronunciation of certain utterances. Drilling would not be used in a literacy class, where speaking activities focus less on accuracy than on clear and coherent self-expression to fit the purpose and the audience.

The underpinning knowledge of how people learn language is relevant for both subjects although, in practice, it is sometimes applied differently. For example, both bilingual and monolingual learners need to understand spelling patterns found in English and develop an awareness of the spelling strategies that can be used. However, the underpinning knowledge of phonology will be applied in literacy to the sound–symbol relationships in written texts, whereas in ESOL it will also be applied to the pronunciation of individual sounds in spoken words and to the understanding of spoken English.

Teachers will still find there are differences between teaching language and teaching literacy because learners will come with different skills and different needs. Literacy learners who are fluent speakers of English have an implicit knowledge of language and language structure; ESOL learners may be fluent in several languages, but they will be less familiar with the structure and vocabulary of English. So, in general, everything that a literacy teacher does might also be done by an ESOL teacher, but an ESOL teacher additionally needs to bear in mind that learners are approaching the English language for the first time and so more clarification on structure and vocabulary of the language will be needed. For example, literacy learners probably don't need to learn the rules of grammar for forming negative statements because they already have an implicit knowledge of how to do this, but they might need to work on other aspects of grammar such as subject–verb agreement. ESOL learners, as well as learning to decode words when reading, might also need help pronouncing words which they may not have encountered before.

FURTHER READING

Hughes, N. and Schwab, I. (2010) *Teaching Adult Literacy: Principles and Practice*. Maidenhead: Open University Press.

Paton, A. and Wilkins, M. (2009) *Teaching Adult ESOL: Principles and Practice*. Maidenhead: Open University Press.

3 The teaching and learning cycle

Irene Schwab

INTRODUCTION

If you google images of 'teacher' you will find dozens of images of a (usually young) man or woman, standing in front of a blackboard or whiteboard talking to groups of learners in a classroom. You don't see the teacher sitting at a computer planning their next session or hunched over a table marking piles of learners' work. Yet these are also crucial parts of a teacher's work and probably take up more time in a teacher's life than the actual delivery of learning in a classroom. In fact, as a new teacher you may spend many hours preparing a lesson that lasts only an hour or so. Later, when you have more teaching experience, preparation may take less time but it will still be a considerable part of your working week. Teaching a class is only a small part of the teacher's role.

Let's look at the process from a learner's point of view. What might their experience be of the process from the first time they arrive at a college or training centre? Some or all of the elements in Figure 3.1 are likely to play a part. The process is sometimes seen as a cycle or a spiral as it continues until the learner decides they have completed their education.

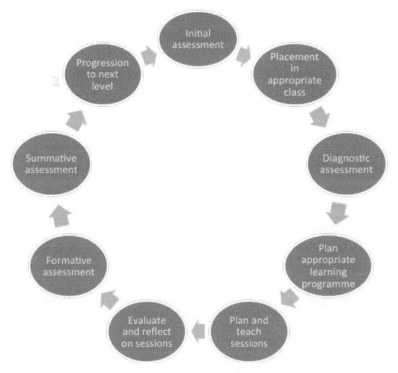

Figure 3.1. The teaching and learning cycle

There are two things we can note here. Firstly, although it is presented as 'the teaching and learning cycle' it is often not a cycle at all but a series of stages, some of which might take place in sequence but which might also take place simultaneously or in a different order.

You will also see from the diagram that many of the nine basic stages involve different types of assessment. Assessment starts at the very beginning of the learner's learning journey and continues throughout:

 》 Identification of learner needs at the start of a programme

 》 Ongoing monitoring and feedback of learning during the course

 》 Assessment at the end of a course

However, all assessment is not the same, even though it might involve using the same or similar materials. What the learner does in each of these stages and why they do it varies considerably. We will look at these stages one by one.

IDENTIFYING NEEDS

When a learner arrives at a college, adult education centre, training provider or even at a prison, they are assessed to find out what their strengths and needs are in relation to language and literacy. This is usually called *initial assessment*. In some institutions it could take the form of three separate assessments:

 》 **Screening:** A quick assessment, maybe taking the form of an interview and/or a quick test (perhaps multiple choice) to see if the applicant needs any form of English class. If they do, they might go on to…

 》 **Initial assessment**: A slightly longer assessment, maybe a more in-depth interview, together with some reading and writing tasks to assess the four skills. The centre might use this assessment to place the learner in a class at an appropriate level for their skills. Many learners have spiky profiles, which means they might be stronger in some of the four skills than in others. The institution will have a policy to place learners according to one or two of the skills, for example speaking or maybe reading and writing English.

 》 **Diagnostic assessment**: This is more detailed again. It is likely to take place in the class to which the learner has been assigned and it may occur over several weeks, forming part of the early teaching sessions. It will give both the teacher and learner a clearer idea of what skills and language knowledge the learner already has and where the gaps might be. A good diagnostic assessment will cover all the key elements of the Core Curriculum and enable the teacher to draw up a profile of the learners in her group.

Whether the institution identifies needs across one assessment or all three, it will help the learner and the teacher to see what they can already do as well as what they need to work on. The teacher can use this information to negotiate realistic and achievable targets with each of the learners. These will be incorporated into an individual learning plan (ILP). Each institution designs its own ILP, a document that sets out individual objectives for each learner on the course. It might also contain group objectives where these are relevant.

DEFINING LEARNING OBJECTIVES/DRAWING UP AN ILP

Some learners are completely clear about why they have enrolled on a course.

) Samira wants to apply for teacher training but has not yet achieved GCSE English, which is a requirement for acceptance on a training course. She needs to improve her written English to get a GCSE grade A*–C.

) Ahmed has just arrived as a refugee in the UK. He has almost no English and needs to be able to communicate as quickly as possible.

) Jessica would like to be able to help her children with their homework now they have reached school age.

) Francisco is on a plumbing apprenticeship and needs to pass Level 1 Functional Skills in English.

) Ling has learned some English in her own country but in formal situations and mainly written English. She now has a job in the UK and needs to be able to communicate with her colleagues.

Other learners might find it more difficult to identify specific objectives, especially if they have not had much schooling previously and are not entirely clear what education involves. Literacy learners might say they just want to learn to read and write well; ESOL learners might indicate that they want to speak English. It is then up to the teacher to investigate further what might be an appropriate course of study for each learner. In Chapter 2 we examined some of the information the teacher will need to find out from each learner.

The teacher will also investigate whether the learner has any support needs or concerns that might affect their ability to pursue the course. These might include the need for childcare, inability to get to the class on time (through work or family commitments), financial or immigration problems or health matters. Most educational providers will have a learner support service, which will be able to offer assistance on these issues better than an individual teacher can, so knowing what is available and how to refer learners is crucial.

In the classroom, the teacher will need to have an awareness of how different disabilities and impairments can impact on learning. If the teacher knows about these, she can rearrange the room, adapt learning activities and materials, amend the learning programme and organise appropriate support where it is needed to support the learner in achieving their objectives. The use of technology can make learning easier for some people but it is important to listen to the learner, as they are likely to know best what will suit their individual needs.

 # TASK 3.1

What do you think a teacher can do to support a learner with these disabilities?

) Visual impairments
) Hearing impairments
) Cognitive disabilities such as dyslexia
) Mental illness

PLANNING AND DESIGNING LEARNING

Once the teacher is clear what the learners want to learn, she can draw up her *scheme of work*. This is her programme for a period of time, maybe half a term, a whole term or a whole year. If the programme is for the whole year, she will have to be prepared to modify and adapt it to changing circumstances throughout the year, according to learner needs. However, she needs to have something to start with so her lessons are staged in a logical sequence, building on previous learning and moving the learners on in small increments.

She needs to bear in mind the end product as well. If there is an exam at the end of the course, she will need to integrate carefully what the learners need to pass the exam (including exam technique) with what they might need more generally. This can cause a tension with some programmes where the exam calls for a particular set of knowledge that she may judge is not what this particular group of learners needs.

The lesson plan

The process of drawing up a scheme of work is discussed in Chapter 7. Here we will look at the more detailed plan for individual lessons – *the lesson plan*. Experienced teachers plan every lesson, even if the plan itself is sometimes quite loose and is not always written down. However, while you are still in training you will be expected to produce a comprehensive written lesson plan for every lesson you teach. Each organisation will have its own proforma for lesson plans but they are all likely to contain the following elements:

1. **Details of date and time of session and teaching room:** If you teach a number of different sessions, this will act as a reminder.

2. **Aims and objectives of the session:** These will help you to be clear about exactly what you expect learners to achieve in the session. The aim is generally what you expect the learners to have learned by the end of the session, whereas the objectives specify what the learner will be able to do as a result of the lesson, describing more detailed stages that will lead to achievement of the aim. Objectives need:

   ❯ A clear outcome

   ❯ A clear range

   ❯ A clear situation or purpose

   For example:

   By the end of the session Tom will be able to:

   - *Use capital letters (outcome) for first names and surnames (range) for members of his family (situation)*

   or

   By the end of the session Tom will be able to:

   - *Write (outcome) a formal letter (range) to complain about his phone bill (purpose)*

The aims and objectives should be selected to help meet the agreed learning goals of the particular group of learners. The acronym SMART is often used to describe learners' goals:

❱ Specific

❱ Measurable

❱ Achievable

❱ Relevant

❱ Time-based

Specific and measurable in relation to targets/tasks; *achievable and relevant* in relation to each individual learner; *time-based* in relation to the lesson or series of lessons.

TASK 3.2

Which of these objectives are specific and measurable?

1. Spell my children's names correctly

2. Write an email to a friend

3. Practise my handwriting

4. Be more confident

5. Proofread a formal letter for spelling mistakes

6. Speak clearly in class

7. Read five signs in college

8. Improve my spelling

9. Use the past simple tense

10. Pick out main points from a chapter in my sociology text book

3. **Teacher and learner activities to be undertaken**: In a good lesson the teacher will be aware of what she is doing, what the learners are doing at any point in the session and what the interaction patterns between them are likely to be.

4. **Timings for activities**: How long have you allowed for each activity? If you overrun, what effect will it have on the rest of the lesson?

5. **What resources will be needed (including ICT):** You need to make sure you have all the resources you need (including enough copies for all learners) and that you have checked that the technology is all in working order.

6. How learning is to be checked: How will you know if the learners have learned what you are trying to teach them?

7. Evaluation of the session: If you teach this session again, what will you need to bear in mind? What will you keep and what might you need to change?

While you are in training it is also a good idea to make a note of your rationale for each session: why you have chosen to teach what you are teaching (language or skills), why you have chosen those particular activities and resources and why you are assessing learning in a particular way. This will help you to evaluate the session afterwards; if you know what you are aiming at it will be easier to see if you have achieved it.

FACILITATING LEARNING

In every session you teach your aim is for learning to take place. There are many different kinds of learning and it can take place in a variety of ways, but if no learning takes place then the session will not have been successful. There are a number of factors that might impact on whether learning happens; some of these are to do with the teacher, some with the learners and some with the learning context. Teacher factors will be directly under your control but you will also have to consider learner factors and the context in which you are teaching for your planning to lead to successful learning.

 TASK 3.3

Are the following *teacher* factors, *learner* factors, or factors relating to the *learning context*?

❱ The lesson plan

❱ Learners' engagement with the topic

❱ The layout of the room

❱ The learning materials

❱ Group dynamics

❱ Communication between teacher and learners

❱ Communication between learners

❱ Clear aims and objectives

❱ Availability of ICT

Remember, talk is work in an ESOL class, so activities involving talk are important. This talk should be predominantly learner talk rather than teacher talk so you need to plan varied patterns of interaction to maximise the opportunities for productive talk. If you have twenty learners in a class and have a whole-group discussion, only one person can talk at a time; if you break the group into five groups of four, then five learners can be talking at any one time; if you set a pair speaking task, then ten learners can be speaking at the same time. That is a great deal more speaking practice for everyone.

When organising activities to promote speaking and listening, you need an awareness of effective ways of promoting constructive talk. Talk can be structured as an activity or can be open and free. In general, shyer learners are more likely to talk in small groups than in whole-group discussions. Consider, also, your use of questioning. Open questions encourage learners to talk more.

Think about how to set up the room for the activities you want to organise. Serried rows are not normally suitable for literacy or ESOL classes. The layout hinders communication as learners cannot see each other's faces. It may also remind them of previous, more formal (and possibly negative), educational experiences. There are a number of options for room layout which promote a more communicative environment:

Learners can be seated around tables, café style:

The tables could form a horseshoe with the teacher and whiteboard at the open end:

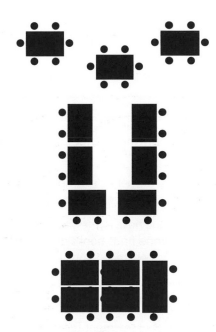

The tables could be pushed together in the centre with everyone sitting around them, boardroom style:

If you are in an IT room, everyone might be seated at a computer:

Remember, you can usually change the seating to suit your group or to facilitate a particular activity. You don't have to stick with whatever has been left in the room by the teacher before you.

Teaching and learning activities

In any one session, it is important to introduce some variety. Even if you know that learners in your group enjoy a particular activity, it will lose its effect if you do it all the time. Try and ensure you have a good mixture, involving:

❭ **Different lengths of time**: A quick warmer activity at the beginning may be useful to revise something learned in a previous session, or as preparation for activities to come. Teachers often find it helpful to offer something brief and engaging that will create interest in the topic. It also means latecomers won't miss the main body of work in the session. On the other hand, you might need to plan a longer period for activities involving writing to allow for the process of planning, drafting and editing and for reading to allow for differences in the speed of silent reading.

❭ **Differentiated activities**, including extension tasks for those who might need less time for reading and writing.

❭ **A mixture of the four skills** (even though you may be focusing on one or two more than the others in any one session).

❭ A combination of **speaking and listening** activities involving different types of interaction.

❭ An assortment of **reading and writing** activities focusing on text, sentence and word-level skills.

❭ **Contextualised practice** using authentic examples of texts and situations that learners are likely to experience in real life.

❭ **Materials that are engaging** and have interesting content and that also cater for different learning preferences. Not everyone finds books appealing. Make use of visual and tactile resources and those that involve new technology (Internet and mobile texts).

Checking learning

We have looked already at the use of assessment techniques to identify learner strengths and development areas. Another use of assessment, and one that is perhaps better known, is to check how effectively the learners have learned what you intended to teach them.

This is important because:

❭ the learner needs feedback on how well they are progressing and to be able to see in which areas they have improved and which they still need to develop;

❭ the teacher needs to see how effective their teaching methods have been; and

❭ both the teacher and learners need to see what still has to be revised or taught.

This checking often takes place at the end of a programme of learning in the form of a test or exam, or maybe a portfolio of work that the learner has completed over the year. It is then called *summative assessment*, being a form of summary of achievement. However, research shows that this needs to happen not just at the end of a course, but all the way through it. This type of ongoing assessment is called *formative assessment* because it moulds the shape of the programme and forms (and informs) the teaching and learning process. Formative assessment is often called assessment *for* learning to distinguish it from summative assessment, which is seen as assessment *of* learning.

Formative assessment is a joint process between teacher and learners and might involve looking at learners' understanding through a variety of processes:

❭ Feedback from teacher to learner

❭ Feedback from learner to teacher

❭ Feedback from learner to other learners (*peer assessment*)

❭ Self-assessment by learners

In this sense it is often difficult to separate out the process of formative assessment from that of good teaching as these processes are all part of effective teaching and learning.

What is essential in formative assessment is for learners to develop the ability to self-monitor and critique the learning process as it applies to themselves. Where learners are working towards a test, encourage them to discuss and evaluate their own assessment criteria. If they are familiar with the constituents of a good answer, it will be easier to reproduce one. Discussing model answers helps understand official and unofficial assessment criteria. Some key aspects of *formative assessment* are:

❭ questioning (by the teacher and the learners) to help clarify the learners' understanding

❭ detailed and constructive feedback on activities

❭ detailed discussion about what works and what doesn't

While it might be motivating for the teacher to feed back to a learner 'Well done, that was a good piece of work', it does not, alone, help them progress further and produce a better piece of work. Even 'Well done, that was a good piece of work but mind your spelling' is not very helpful as it is not precise enough. Aim for comments that show appreciation of what the learner has achieved, but which also give them clear and detailed assistance in what they have to do to improve, such as:

Well done, you described your home village clearly. I can get a clear picture of what it looked like. Don't forget that a sense of place is also created by the use of the other senses: What can you hear? What can you smell? What does it feel like when you touch certain things? Are there any particular tastes that it makes you remember? Try and bring these into your writing.

These might be written or oral comments. With some learners you can have a dialogue about their understanding of certain aspects of learning; with others, whose level of English might hamper such a dialogue, there are tools that can be used to help them feed back to the teacher. For example, a traffic lights system used with coloured cards, post-its, or even paper cups for quick feedback. Learners are each given a set of cards and can hold up the relevant one so the teacher can see at a glance how many of the group need more help. Green means the learner feels confident that he understands; orange, he partly understands but needs more practice; and red, he doesn't understand.

EVALUATING TEACHING AND LEARNING

If a lesson goes well, it is important to think about what elements contributed to its success, so that they can be repeated. If it doesn't go so well, then the teacher needs to think about what went wrong and how she can avoid that happening again. In most cases there will be aspects of the lesson that went well and others that were less successful. In order to develop as a teacher you should evaluate every lesson to explore the reasons behind both and treat the process as a learning opportunity. This is the core of *reflective practice*.

Kolb (1984) represented this process as a cycle:

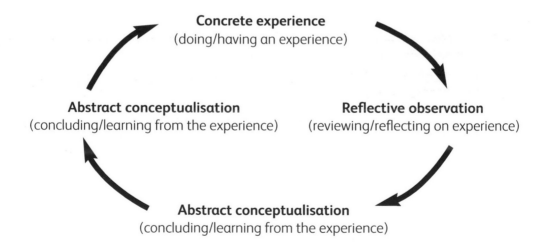

Concrete experience
(doing/having an experience)

Reflective observation
(reviewing/reflecting on experience)

Abstract conceptualisation
(concluding/learning from the experience)

Abstract conceptualisation
(concluding/learning from the experience)

He argued that we start with a concrete experience (in this case a lesson). And we reflect on how it went (reflective observation) leading to a generalisation of what has to be done to improve practice (abstract conceptualisation). We then try and do something different in our next session (active experimentation). The cycle then begins again when we try out something new the following session.

Reflection does not need to be a complex process. You can provide some simple headings to help yourself with the thinking:

❱ What did I do that went well?

❱ What did I do that didn't go so well?

❱ What can I do to improve a session like this if I teach it again?

The crucial question here is how can you tell if the session went well? You might ask yourself:

❱ Did I achieve my lesson objectives (i.e. did the learners learn what I intended them to learn)?

❱ Did the learners learn anything else (unplanned learning)?

❱ If they did learn, what helped them with the learning?

❱ If they didn't learn, what hindered their learning?

❱ Did every learner gain something from the lesson? If some didn't, why not?

Of course, none of this will be possible unless you have checked learning effectively during the session. Formative assessment, if done correctly, will have given both you and the learners some idea of how well they were learning at each point in the session. Your evaluation of the lesson should feed into your planning for the next session, thus starting the teaching and learning cycle again.

FURTHER READING

Black, P. *et al.* (2003) *Assessment for Learning: Putting It Into Practice.* Milton Keynes: Open University Press.

Hughes, N. and Schwab, I. (2010) *Teaching Adult Literacy: Principles and Practice.* Maidenhead: Open University Press.

Paton, A. and Wilkins, M. (2009) *Teaching Adult ESOL: Principles and Practice.* Maidenhead: Open University Press.

4 Teaching practice

David Mallows

INTRODUCTION

Watching an experienced teacher at work can be a frustrating experience for those new to the profession – it all looks so effortless, so natural. But it isn't. Learning to teach takes time, patience, reflection, and a lot of practice. It is through the teaching practice element of your course that you will be able to begin your development as a teacher. Teaching practice is where you get the chance to apply everything discussed in the other chapters of this book and that you will learn about in the input sessions on your course.

You will come across lots of theoretical ideas about teaching: theories of learning, of literacy development, of second language acquisition, of group interaction. You will also hear (and hold) lots of opinions about teaching and teachers. We've all been in classrooms as learners and bring with us strong ideas about what a teacher should be. However, bear in mind that there's no such thing as an ideal teacher and there's no correct way to teach. Every teacher is different and what works for one person may not work in the same way for another. Teaching practice is your chance to find your own teaching style.

WHAT IS TEACHING PRACTICE?

Teaching practice can be organised in a number of different ways, but the basic structure is the same. You will be expected to teach a group of learners for a specified time while being observed. You will also be expected to plan the teaching and prepare any resources to be used. Following the class you will be asked to reflect on your teaching and you will be given feedback by the observer(s).

The course that you take may use one or a combination of the following models of teaching practice.

Individual teaching practice

Using this model, the trainee teacher works alone with a group of learners, observed by a teaching practice mentor. It will likely include an initial element of shadowing the existing teacher, your mentor, but you should quickly assume full responsibility for planning, teaching and assessing the learners. This model is closer to everyday professional practice, in effect, although you will be closely supervised by your mentor, you will have your own class and take responsibility for teaching the group.

Group teaching practice

With this model, you share a group of learners with three to six other trainee teachers, taking turns to teach a part of each lesson, observed by your peers and the teacher trainer. You then meet immediately after the taught session to reflect and evaluate the class. Everyone contributes to collaborative formative discussions and you get oral feedback from both the trainer and your peers. You also get to contribute to the evaluation of your peers' teaching. This collaborative approach and shared experience is a key advantage of the group teaching practice model. As you are all teaching the same class you can learn a lot from watching your peers teach. The trainer will expect you to observe carefully (often using a specific observation task) and contribute actively to the feedback session, so make sure you are an active observer, asking yourself questions as you watch. What is the teacher trying to do? Do the learners understand what the teacher is trying to do? Do all of the learners react in the same way? During feedback on the teaching of one of your colleagues, the trainer will often make a general point about teaching that is as applicable to you and your development as a teacher as it is your colleague.

You also benefit from co-planning the teaching practice with your peers and trainer. Your trainer will ensure you try out different methods and cover a range of subject knowledge in the sessions that you teach. It is also possible for the trainer to model techniques with the training group and for the trainees to observe more experienced teachers teaching the group.

Paired teaching practice

Paired teaching practice is something of a halfway stage between the two models outlined above. With this model, two trainees share responsibility for teaching a single group of learners at a placement organisation supervised by the teacher normally responsible for the group. You may teach alternately, observing one another, or sometimes you will take half the learners each, dividing the room in two. You will provide support for each other, sharing reflections based on knowledge of the same learners. You will work under the supervision of the class teacher, who will help you to learn from your teaching practice through co-operative planning, informal feedback and discussion. As with the individual model, you will play a gradually increasing role in planning, supported by the class teacher, and you will receive feedback from the class teacher as a 'critical friend'. You will also receive some peer feedback from your partner. Formal observations for the purposes of assessment are usually carried out during periodic visits by the trainer.

WHAT TO THINK ABOUT BEFORE TEACHING

As well as actually teaching a group of learners you will need to produce certain documents, such as a rationale for the lesson, a lesson plan and a profile of the learners in the group. The format for these will depend on the requirements of the course and/or the place in which you are teaching. These are important documents and you should be aware that they will take time to complete. However, this will be time well spent. Even if things don't go to plan once you actually teach the lesson, a well-constructed lesson plan demonstrates to your tutor that you are able to plan a lesson appropriately. Similarly the learner profiles and rationale give you the opportunity to show that you are thinking about the learners as individuals, each with their own learning needs, and have selected activities and materials that are appropriate to the learners and their stage of learning.

When you first begin teaching you will feel as though every move you make is being scrutinised and judged, that every word you say is being closely analysed and that far too much is being read into the gestures you make and the expressions that flash across your face. Even the most confident and extrovert among you will feel self-conscious, awkward and, at times, that you would far rather be somewhere else. This is normal. In learning to teach most people move from a concern early in the course with looking like a teacher, with comments relating to their voice and confidence, to a later concern with the teaching process and the activities chosen, and then to whether learning has taken place. This shift in perspective on what is important in teaching can be seen as a progression from a focus on the teacher, to the materials and activities being used, and finally to the learners and their learning. In early teaching practice sessions you and your fellow trainees will likely be very concerned with the image of a teacher that you present to the learners. As the course progresses and you gain more experience you will be able to focus less on yourself and your success (or otherwise) in acting like a teacher and more on the teaching itself, and subsequently on the learners and their learning.

So, be aware that you will feel self-conscious, but also be aware that you are not the most important person in the room. It really isn't all about you and the sooner you focus your attention on the learners and their learning the better. You will find that once you do this and you begin to engage with the learners in front of you and hear them respond to your prompts, answer your questions, and even smile and laugh a little, you will relax, time will fly and you will be reminded why you are training to teach literacy and ESOL.

Scripting instructions

Teaching is unpredictable and you can't plan the questions that your learners will ask you, nor do you know how they will react to the prompts and activities you have planned. However, there are certain elements that you can pre-plan in detail, giving you more confidence and ensuring that you are able to focus on the learners rather than on your lesson plan. One of these elements is instruction. It doesn't matter how interesting and useful your activities are if the learners don't know what to do. Explaining what you want learners to do may seem quite straightforward but it is often far from it, as many trainees (and experienced teachers) have found to their cost. One way to avoid blank looks on learners' faces and the ensuing confusion and delay as you attempt to repair the damage, is to script your instructions in advance. There are a number of principles that you should bear in mind when thinking about how to introduce an activity.

> **Keep it simple and direct:** Remember that these are instructions. You know what you want learners to do and you need to tell them to do that. And just that.

> **Don't try to be excessively polite:** Make use of imperatives and don't embed your instructions. It is far easier for learners to understand a simple command of:

Open your books to page ten.

than:

Would you mind getting your books out, if you could, and then open them to page, erm, ten I think it was… . Yes, page ten please. Thanks.

❭ **On a need-to-know basis:** Only tell learners what they need to know to carry out the next task. If you want them to discuss a picture, then read an article, then do some language work before writing a description of the picture for homework – for now, just tell them to discuss the picture.

❭ **Check** that they have understood before telling them to begin. Doing an example together is usually a good way to clarify what to learners have to do, as are check questions such as:

'What exercise are you going to do?'

'How many examples do you need?'

'Are you going to write anything?'

TASK 4.1

Look at these extracts from a lesson plan and write out exactly what you would ask learners to do.

	Time	Stage aims	Teacher activity	Resources
1	20 minutes	Find and identify commonly used words in job adverts	Give out page of job ads and related task (Identify the jobs advertised. Then highlight adjectives – job or candidate?) Highlight other new vocabulary and discuss meaning. Monitor, guide weaker learners. Feedback. Concept check and drill new vocabulary	Jobs page from Skills for Life Literacy Entry 2 learner materials.
2	15 minutes	To practise extracting relevant information	Ask learners to listen to the interview and see if any of the questions on the board are asked – make a quick note of the numbers of the questions that you hear that are that are similar to or the same as the Qs you hear	Tracks 48 and 49

Routines

When you observe an experienced teacher you will notice that they do certain things the same way each time, for example when they are setting up pair work, eliciting vocabulary or checking learners' answers. All teachers build a store of routines that they draw on consistently to handle the repetitive features of classroom activity. Such instructional routines are strategies of teaching that teachers have developed over time and use at regular points in the course of a lesson in regular configurations and sequences. A simple example is the use of pair checking followed by whole-class feedback on completion of individual exercises. An experienced teacher doesn't have to plan what will happen when learners have completed an exercise, thinking through the desired interactions or how to word instructions; instead, a routine is deployed.

Developing a series of simple routines is very helpful when you are beginning to teach. You will be doing something you are unaccustomed to, trying out new ideas in an unfamiliar setting and everyone will be looking at you. Both ESOL and literacy classrooms are complex places – learners bring with them a wide variety of expectations based on their own experience of classrooms, they will have differing learning needs and react in different ways to everything that you do. For the teacher there is an enormous amount of information to be collected, processed, analysed and acted upon. Under these circumstances having a number of simple routines that you can follow without much thought will be a great help, freeing you up to notice more of what is happening in the classroom, allowing you to learn from learners' reactions and responses.

WHAT TO THINK ABOUT WHILE YOU ARE TEACHING

There is a lot going on at all times in the language and literacy classroom. You need to listen to learners and understand what they are saying (or want to say). You need to be aware of the social interactions in the classroom and judge the mood of the learners: who is paying attention, who has lost concentration, who is annoyed with whom, and so on. And you need to do this constantly, while at the same time remembering what you have just done, planning what you are going to do next, responding to learners' questions and comments, and watching the clock to make sure you are on track to achieve your aims in the time available.

Good teachers listen carefully to learners, gathering data on their language use, their mood, their interactions with other learners and many other things. They then use this data to guide their actions. In this way they can act in a purposeful way in the classroom, making informed decisions about the activities that they plan and their interventions during the class. In your teaching you should aim for *purposefulness*. That is, you should do what you do based on analysis of the interactions of a number of different factors: the language used, the source of any errors or misunderstandings, the social situation, the emotional response of learners and many others. Such analysis needs to be carried out quickly and accurately, as the results inform the decisions that the teacher takes. For example, in an ESOL class, while listening to learners talk the teacher needs to weigh up a number of factors that will inform what action she takes:

Should I intervene while the learner is speaking to correct an error?

What should the focus of my intervention be – the vocabulary, the pronunciation, the grammar? All three?

In making these decisions the teacher needs to draw on a great deal of linguistic knowledge:

> ❯ to identify an error (or a correct piece of language that you may want to highlight for other learners);

> ❯ to make some informed hypotheses about why the learner may have made that error – is it to do with their level or have they confused it with something else? It might also be just a slip rather than the result of a misunderstanding or lack of knowledge; and

> ❯ to be able to see connections between the language item/structure in question and other items/structures in order to help the learner develop a holistic understanding of the language and to accelerate their learning.

To make such decisions on the hoof in front of a class of adults requires a principled understanding of the types of interactions, linguistic and social, that make up the activities of the classroom. Above all, it requires you to be focused on the learners and their learning rather than on yourself and what you are doing.

Teaching practice is your best opportunity to study the classroom to better understand what happens and why so that you can focus on learning rather than teaching. There are a number of simple things that you can do that will help you to feel more confident and enable you to focus less on what you are doing and more on the learners and their learning.

Teacher position

You should always be conscious of your position in the classroom, as it has an effect on your ability to control the class and to communicate effectively with the learners. Where you stand in the classroom has an impact on the interaction between you and the learners in the group. On a very simple level you should make sure that when you are speaking all of the learners can see you speak – check that you can make eye contact with everyone.

There are four simple positions that you can take in the classroom.

> ❯ You can stand at the front of the class – this is good for setting up activities, giving explanations and instructions. Make sure you are in the middle and that no one is behind you (you can check this by holding your arms out wide in front of you – is the whole group 'inside' your arms? If not, move back). When you are at the front of the class it can be very tempting to drift in towards the learner who has just made a comment or asked a question. Don't. Remember that even when addressing a comment or question from an individual learner, your job is to involve the whole group, and by drifting in you limit the possibility of interaction with, and between, other learners.

> ❯ Moving from this position at the front of the group to the board signals that you want learners to focus on something that you are going to write there. When you are at the board, try to avoid talking to it! Even when you are writing something, if you want to speak you need to make sure that you turn to face the class – it's very easy to forget to turn round and very hard for learners to follow what you are saying if they can't see your face. It's also impossible for you to tell if they are listening if you aren't looking at them.

❭ Try not to wander around too much at the front of the class – it can be distracting for learners and makes it more difficult for them to follow what you say.

❭ You are also allowed to sit down. If you want to have a discussion with learners or to get them to tell you and the class about themselves, then sit down – if you met friends in a café and they were sitting at a table, you might say a brief hello while standing up, but to engage in a proper conversation you would likely join them and sit down. The same applies with teaching. By sitting down you place yourself on the same level as the rest of the group, signalling that you are not talking to them as you did when you were standing at the front giving instructions or when you were at the board explaining something. Instead you are one of the group and plan to engage in a conversation. Sitting down in this way (again, make sure that you choose a position where everyone can see you) also makes it far more likely that you will be able to encourage learners to talk to each other rather than just to you.

❭ In both literacy and ESOL classes you will also need to spend time working one to one with learners. This will require you to join them at their table to check their work, help them if they are stuck, and discuss what they are doing. You need to think carefully about your approach, but where possible you should try to work beside the learners rather than in front as this facilitates sharing of the text. You also need to decide whether to crouch down or sit; much will depend on the layout of the room. Avoid leaning over the learners wherever possible as this can be uncomfortable for them.

Eye contact

You should try to engage all of the learners in the group. One of your key tools to do this is eye contact. Make sure that you look learners in the eye as you speak and while you listen to them. They will feel more involved and be more likely to contribute, and you will be better able to judge their mood and see how they are reacting to your teaching and to each other. Make sure that you include everyone, don't just focus on those who are more responsive; constantly scan the room to encourage everyone to listen and respond. When you scan the room don't just look mechanically from left to right – that way the learners will get used to your movements and only pay attention when they feel your eyes approaching. Think of the classroom as the five on a dice and make sure your eyes hit all five points, but in no particular order.

Eye contact is very important when you want to engage the whole class or an individual learner, but when they are working in pairs or in groups be careful not to make eye contact or their attention will be drawn to you, away from the person you want them to engage with.

Voice

You are likely to be nervous when you first teach and those nerves may well manifest themselves in the volume and clarity of your voice. Firstly, make sure that the learners can hear you. Project your voice to the back of the room, but don't shout. Speak clearly (no mumbling), but naturally. You will have to grade your language in the ESOL classroom. This means selecting language items that are appropriate to the level of the learners – for example, no colloquialisms or complex sentence structures with beginners. But you should not attempt to speak very slowly or place equal stress on every syllable. For example it is common for new teachers to try to avoid contractions by asking, 'What is your name?' rather than, 'What's your name?' and place equal stress on each word. This does the learners no favours. Not only does it provide them with a false model to copy, It also makes it more difficult for them to understand people outside the classroom, as they will not speak in this way. You should always provide a clear but natural model for learners.

Nomination

It's amazing what a difference knowing learners' names can make. Aim to say everyone's name at least once during the lesson – it will put the learners at ease, signalling that you think of them as individuals rather than generic learners. When you teach the group, nominate learners when you ask a question and use their names as much as possible.

When you are first observing the class that you are going to teach, set yourself the task of learning everyone's names. Not only will this help you to think about them as individuals, it will also make it easier for you to remember the things that they say, their interests and personalities – all of which will help you when planning. If you haven't yet memorised their names when you first get up in front of them, ask everyone to put their name on a folded piece of paper on their desk.

Gestures

You should develop a limited set of fixed gestures that your learners come to recognise and respond to. Use these consistently and clearly to convey meaning or to give instructions. When you observe other teachers you should note down the gestures that they use and try them out for yourself. However, any gesture you adopt should feel natural to you (once you have tried it a few times), there are no right or wrong ways to do this and your gestures will develop over time. For example, most teachers point over their shoulder to mark past time, but the way in which they do this differs greatly. The important thing to remember is that your gestures should be clear and consistent.

 TASK 4.2

What gestures would you use to signal that learners should:

❯ stop talking/working?

❯ work in pairs?

❯ listen to you?

What gestures would you use to:

❯ mark the stressed syllable in a word?

❯ indicate the past or future tense?

Making the most of feedback

As soon as you have finished teaching you should begin reflecting on how it went. Your tutor will probably ask you to make some notes that he or she will use to shape the oral and written feedback that you will receive. The format and particular headings for this will differ depending on the course, but the things you are likely to be asked to think about include the following.

❭ Overall impression: In general how did it go? What went well, what needs further consideration and what will you take forward into your future practice?

❭ The aims: Did you achieve them?

❭ Classroom management: Did you manage to create a positive and purposeful learning environment? Did learners always know what to do and why they were being asked to do it?

❭ The learners' reactions: Were they engaged at all times?

❭ Communication: How effectively were you able to get your message across to the learners?

❭ Timing: Which parts of the lesson overran and which took less time than you expected?

❭ Differentiation: How did you cater for the different learning needs of the learners?

Try to approach feedback in a positive way. No class is perfect – there is always something that could have been done better and there are many different ways to do the same thing. Feedback is your chance to engage in a constructive discussion with your tutor, mentor or fellow trainees and reflect on what went well and which aspects of your teaching practice require further development.

OBSERVING OTHER TEACHERS

One of the best ways to learn more about teaching is to watch other teachers in action. Observing other teachers will help you to reflect on your own teaching and give you ideas that you can incorporate into your own teaching. Every teacher has copied someone else at some stage of their learning to teach. While observing you should be actively seeking things that you can try out yourself.

Before you begin the observation, decide what you want to focus on. It's a good idea to use an observation to look carefully at something that you find particularly challenging, such as giving instructions, leading a classroom discussion, correcting pronunciation, or using the board. Make a point of noting down how the teacher you're observing approaches this.

It can be tempting to focus entirely on classroom management, as this is the most visible aspect of any lesson, but try to also look at other aspects of the lesson, such as the lesson plan, the staging of activities, the interaction patterns among learners and particularly the learning outcomes – are learners 'getting it'? Is there any evidence that they can do something better at the end of the lesson than before?

Don't just watch the teacher. You should pay close attention to the reactions and behaviour of the learners. Seeing the class from their perspective will help you to better understand their reactions to things you do in class.

A good exercise to carry out after you have observed another teacher is to try to reconstruct the lesson plan from your notes and to think through what the aims of each activity are, how they relate to each other and form a coherent whole lesson and why the teacher has ordered them in this way.

And it isn't just experienced teachers that you can learn from. Carefully observing your fellow trainees is also an excellent way to gain greater insight into the complex environment of the classroom.

WORKING WITH YOUR MENTOR

If you have a placement as part of your course then you will also likely be assigned to a mentor. This is an experienced teacher in the organisation in which you carry out your placement. Your mentor is there to help you develop your subject knowledge and teaching practice; he or she will provide teaching and subject-specific expertise and support. While you are on your placement, your mentor should encourage you to develop your reflective skills by offering advice and guidance, undertaking teaching observations and offering written feedback that identifies your strengths and development needs. Your mentor should give you plenty of support at first, but will gradually withdraw it as you become more confident and competent.

The mentor may also provide information on subject-specific teaching methods, syllabi and specifications, schemes of work and/or examinations. They may help you access general or subject specific department resources and they should also endeavour to ensure that your practical needs are met – *Where's the photocopier? How do I work the projector? What time do they have a break?*

This is a different role to that of the tutor you will have on the course, but their approach to teaching and the advice they give you should be complementary. Take every opportunity to observe your mentor teaching and, above all, ask as many questions as you can, about what you have seen them do in class, about the materials they use, the scheme of work, the individual learners. Most teachers enjoy discussing teaching and the more you ask (and the better you listen), the more you will learn.

FURTHER READING

Gower, R., Walters, S. and Phillips, D. (1995) *Teaching Practice Handbook*. London: Macmillan.

Harmer, J, (2007) 'Managing learning', in id. *How to Teach English: An Introduction to the Practice of English Language Teaching* (2nd edn). London: Longman.

Scrivener, J. (2011) 'Classroom management', in id. *Learning Teaching* (3rd edn). London: Macmillan.

5 Language knowledge

Jane Allemano

INTRODUCTION

As a teacher of both ESOL and literacy you will be, essentially, a teacher of English as a language. For ESOL learners this is the main reason for coming to classes; for some it is the only reason, others may have literacy needs as well. On the other hand, literacy learners may well be fluent users of English but want to improve the range of language at their disposal as well as their reading and writing skills in the language. In all cases, as teachers you will need a sound knowledge of how the language is constructed and used. The English language is an enormous subject and so the aim of this chapter can only be to get you started. In this chapter we will look at the key areas that you should focus on to begin with and you will develop your knowledge further through your teaching. In fact, you will continue to learn throughout your career.

It is important to remember that you will not need to teach learners all of the information in this chapter directly. However, it is important for you to have the knowledge to inform the way you guide and feed back to your learners.

As a framework for describing language we can talk about word, sentence and whole-text 'level'. It is important to ensure that there is focus on all three of these in any ESOL or literacy course.

WORD LEVEL

We will begin with words, otherwise known as vocabulary or lexis. We all need words – ESOL learners may have very few English words when they start their course, but all learners of literacy and ESOL will benefit from extending their lexicon, or bank of words that they have at their disposal. In fact, people at all levels of education can learn more.

There is a big difference between understanding a word and being able to use it – the meaning is only the beginning.

There is a lot that we need to know about a word:

> ❱ **Word class:** Is it a noun, verb, adjective, adverb, preposition, or determiner? (We will cover these in more detail later in the chapter.)

> ❱ **Meaning:** Some words have different meanings in different contexts. For example, a *table* in a room, a *table* in a text and *tables* in mathematics; *take some medicine* and *take your umbrella with you*. Also, some words mean one thing as a noun and another as a verb or adjective, for example *a fair* versus *to be fair…* Some words can have a figurative meaning and are not always used in their literal meaning – for example, *it's boiling outside* means it very hot, not 100 degrees centigrade.

> ❱ **Connotation:** This is an element of meaning. Some words have a positive or negative tone, for example *slim* is more positive than *skinny*.

❯ **Collocation:** This refers to the way words are used together. This may not directly translate from other languages: for example, to be interested *in* doing something but keen *on* doing something; a *high* mountain but a *tall* person.

❯ **Register:** Some words are informal, such as *pal* or *mate*, and others are more neutral or formal, such as *friend* or *acquaintance*.

❯ **Morphology:** You can change the word to make it negative or change the word class (see the next section) by adding to the beginning or end of the word. For example, *attract, attractive, unattractive, attracted, attractively.*

❯ **Syntax:** This refers to the way a word can affect the syntax of the rest of the sentence, for example *pay me* but *give it to me, enjoy doing* but *want to do* (for more about this see the section on lexico-grammatical features). Some verbs need an object, for example *you buy something*, and others do not, for example *he is working* can stand alone.

❯ **Pronunciation:** This includes the sounds of the vowels and consonants and knowing the stressed syllable, for example *impor**tant*** has a strong stress on the second syllable.

❯ **Spelling:** English spelling is not regular – the same sound can be spelled in several different ways. For example, words that rhyme with 'air' (where, bear, fare, their, they're, Claire, mayor, layer) can be spelled in at least nine ways. This means that learning spelling is an important part of language and literacy learning.

 TASK 5.1

a) Consider the word '*eccentric*' in the sentence below and fill in the table

The most <u>eccentric</u> person I know goes everywhere on an ancient bicycle decorated with flowers.

Word class	
Meaning(s)	
Connotation	
Register	
Pronunciation	
Collocation	
Morphology	

b) Now take the word '*patient*' and make a list of everything you know about this word.

As we have seen, words can be broken down into smaller units. These units are called *phonemes* and *morphemes*. Phonemes are the individual sounds of English – the vowels and consonants. These are important for pronunciation and spelling. Some pairs of words differ by only one phoneme, such as work/walk, live/leave, night/might, meet/met (see the section in this chapter on phonology).

Morphemes are the smallest units that carry meaning or grammatical function, for example *prefixes* and *suffixes*. With these, we can alter or add to words to make opposites, add extra information or change the word class. Most longer words have a *root*, which is the part that carries the basic meaning. Take for example the word 'comfort': this can be used as a noun or a verb but it also forms the root of 'uncomfortable'. Sometimes the root changes slightly when a prefix or suffix is added, for example 'conclude/conclusion'. It is useful for both ESOL and literacy learners to look at word formation in this way so that they can increase the range of language at their disposal.

 TASK 5.2

Can you identify the root of the following words?

❱ Needlessly

❱ Systemically

❱ Disqualified

❱ Dirtiest

❱ Illogical

PREFIXES

A **prefix** is attached to the beginning of a word to change its meaning: for example, *dis, un, il, im, in, non* all make opposites:

❱ appear – *dis*appear

❱ usual – *un*usual

❱ legal – *il*legal

❱ polite – *im*polite

❱ significant – *in*significant

❱ native – *non*-native

TASK 5.3

What do the prefixes *re, extra, under, inter, over, mis, mid, pre, post,* and *anti* mean? Can you think of nouns, verbs and adjectives we might add them to?

SUFFIXES

We often change the word class by adding a *suffix* to the ends of words. Formal language usually contains more nouns than informal language so learners can change their register more easily if they know how to convert a verb into a noun. For example, 'When you arrive…' is more informal than 'On arrival…'.

TASK 5.4

a) What could be added to these verbs and adjectives to make them nouns?

❭ Arrive
❭ Employ
❭ Work
❭ Bore
❭ Child
❭ Train
❭ Depend
❭ Happy
❭ Liable
❭ Attract
❭ Invite

Can you think of other nouns with the same suffixes?

b) What could be added to these verbs and nouns to make adjectives?

❭ Read
❭ Snow
❭ Beauty
❭ Wire
❭ Tropic
❭ Fame
❭ Attract

Can you think of other adjectives with the same suffixes?

Set phrases are groups of words that are frequently used in the same combinations. A lot of social pleasantries come into this category ('How are you?', 'See you soon', 'Nice to meet you') and so do idioms, where the meaning may be figurative – 'a drop in the ocean', 'a little bird told me', 'a piece of cake'. These are examples of fixed expressions, that is, they do not change, whereas other expressions are semi-fixed, such as 'Would you mind if I... smoked/opened the window?', 'Could you please pass me the salt/pepper/butter?' (Lewis, 2002). As with single lexical items there can be register and connotation issues with these expressions.

TASK 5.5

Consider the idiom 'a taste of your own medicine'. How would you advise a learner about its use in terms of register, collocation and connotation?

Even if words are not part of set phrases, they are rarely used in isolation except for a command like 'Stop!' or a short response: 'Yes', 'No', 'Great!'

In order to become part of a sentence, words may become grammaticalised. All words belong to a word class and each word class has a role in a sentence. We saw earlier how we can use suffix morphemes to change word class; we can also use them to change the grammatical function of a word:

Nouns:	add -s, -es, -en to form plurals
Adjectives:	add -er, -est to form comparatives and superlatives
Verbs:	add -s
	add -ed
	add -ing

TASK 5.6

Think for a minute about the functions of these suffixes.

-s

-ed

-ing

-en

When do we use each of them with verbs?

Words used in sentences can also affect the words that come after or before them.

TASK 5.7

Look at the following text and fill in the gaps with the appropriate word.

I had never paid much attention ___ history at school because I was never very good ___ it but when I grew __ I was interested __ finding out more about the origins ___ the town where I lived.

What do all the missing words have in common?

The words that you needed for these gaps are all *prepositions*. In these sentences they combine with the verbs, nouns and adjectives that they follow. We are always interested *in* something (or *doing* something), we are good *at* certain sports or activities. ESOL learners find these prepositions very difficult to learn as in other languages very often different prepositions are used.

Prepositions are also frequently combined with verbs. However, whereas in a combination like 'sit down' or 'grow up' the words keep the same meaning together as they do separately, some verb/preposition combinations change the meaning of the original words. For example, *to put someone up* or *to get round to doing something*. These are called *phrasal verbs* and are very common in informal English. Unfortunately, they are very difficult for ESOL learners to understand and to learn. It is important to be aware that if you use too many of these verbs when speaking to non-native speakers you may not be understood.

There are dictionaries of phrasal verbs which some learners buy and try to study but it is usually more successful if they learn these verbs and their attendant structures as they encounter them in a memorable context.

Another issue that ESOL learners find difficult is whether certain verbs or adjectives are followed by:

❭ the **infinitive** (base form), for example 'I want to go', 'I am happy to go'; or

❭ the **–ing** form, for example 'I love living by the sea', 'I'm keen on going to the cinema'.

Some verbs can be followed by either the infinitive or the –ing form but the meaning changes: for example, *try, stop*, and *remember*.

TASK 5.8

What are the differences in the meaning of the verbs in the following pairs of sentences?

❱ Bill is **trying** to lose weight

❱ He has **tried** going to the gym more often

❱ Steve has **stopped** smoking at last

❱ He **stopped** to talk to me

❱ Jill **remembers** sitting on her grandmother's knee as a child

❱ Please **remember** to post this on your way home.

A good learners' dictionary will give the grammatical patterns used with lexical items. It is good practice to encourage learners to record new words along with their grammatical structures, for example they should not just write down 'advise' but 'to advise somebody to do something'.

SENTENCE LEVEL

Every complete sentence has a verb. The verb system of a language is important for ESOL learners to become familiar with and it is very important for teachers of ESOL and literacy to have a sound knowledge of it in order to teach, correct and guide their learners. Many literacy learners may speak a variety of English which uses some verb forms differently. It is good practice to help them to be aware of different ways of using language in order to allow them to make choices about how they use language in different situations, for example in a formal letter or an email to a friend. Discussion about different varieties, their use and their relative status is helpful for learners in making these decisions.

Tenses

The word *tense* is often used to describe the grammatical structures, involving verb forms, which refer to time. Learning to use tenses correctly is an important part of language learning and is likely to be prominent in your scheme of work for an ESOL class. It is important to realise that while some languages have tenses that seem similar in form, they can be used differently, and that some languages do not use tenses at all.

Time is one important factor to consider when thinking about English verbs – is the action in the present or the past? However, we also need to consider aspect. In English we have *simple*, *perfect* and *continuous aspects*, which, in combination with time, give us the tense forms with which we are familiar.

PRESENT		PAST	
Simple present *I play* *I drive*	**Present perfect** *I have played* *I have driven*	**Simple past** *I played* *I drove*	**Past perfect** *I had played* *I had driven*
Present continuous *I am playing* *I am driving*	**Present perfect continuous** *I have been playing* *I have been driving*	**Past continuous** *I was playing* *I was driving*	**Past perfect continuous** *I had been playing* *I had been driving*

When we teach these tenses, it is important to remember to teach the question and negative forms and that the verb form may change for I, he/she, we/you/they. For example, 'I play' but 'He plays', 'I was playing' but 'You *were* playing'. This is known as *subject/verb agreement* and learners find this difficult, especially when the subject is separated from the verb, for example 'The reason for the changes is quite simple.' Here 'the reason' is the subject so the verb is singular – 'is'.

Future

There are number of ways in which we talk about the future. It is often assumed that the future tense in English is the form 'will' + 'verb' and, while we do use this construction to talk to predict what we think will happen in the future ('England will not win the World Cup') or to announce a spontaneous decision ('I'll get the door') or promise ('I'll make it up to you'), there are a number of other ways in which we talk about the future:

> ❭ 'What time is your train tomorrow?' (Present simple used for timetabled events in the future)

> ❭ 'We're travelling on the same plane next month' (Present continuous used to speak about future plans)

> ❭ 'I'm going to work harder next year' (Going to + verb used to talk about future intentions)

It's important to think carefully about how they differ and which order you would teach them in.

Time and tense

Time and tense do not always match; present tenses can be used for past or future actions and vice versa. For example, 'I'm leaving at six tomorrow' uses a present tense (the present continuous – 'I'm leaving') but refers to the future: 'tomorrow'. Similarly, 'It's time we went' uses a past tense (the past simple – 'went') but refers to the present (the time is not stated, but is understood as 'now').

TASK 5.9

What tense are the following verbs in bold and what time do they refer to?

	Tense	Time
I would rather you **didn't smoke** in here		
I wish I **had** more free time		
I **was wondering** if you could lend me a tenner		
The film **starts** at 8.30pm		

Modality

Modal verbs are verbs that we combine with other verbs to express:

❱ likelihood – *will, might, may, can, could, must*

❱ ability – *can, could*

❱ permission – *can, could*

❱ obligation/recommendation – *must, should*

You will notice that some of these verbs appear under more than one category.

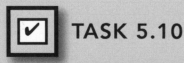

TASK 5.10

Match the modal verbs underlined with the uses listed above.

❱ 'They're very late. They <u>must (1)</u> have got lost. I think you <u>should (2)</u> call and ask them.'

❱ 'I <u>can't (3)</u> do that; there's no reception here.'

❱ 'Try across the road; you <u>should (4)</u> get a signal there.'

❱ 'I <u>might (5)</u>, I suppose'

Semi-modals

In addition there are a series of semi-modals, such as 'used to' (to refer to a past state or habit that is no longer happening) and 'going to' (to refer to a future intention or fairly certain prediction) which are outside the tense system but are nevertheless used to refer to time.

Simple and compound sentences

Every sentence needs a main clause. The main clause carries the main meaning of a sentence and will still make sense if other parts of the sentence are removed. It must contain a *finite* verb, which means a verb that shows the time it refers to.

In this section we will look at different ways of expanding sentences in order to help ESOL and literacy learners increase the sophistication of their writing.

Look at this simple sentence:

John	cooked	the supper
I	I	I
Subject	Verb	Object

There are two nouns in this sentence: *John* and *supper*. We might want to find out more about the supper:

❱ John cooked *a delicious supper*

Or even more:

❱ John cooked *a delicious supper using leftovers.*

Also, we might want more information about John:

❱ *Rose's partner, John, cooked a delicious supper using leftovers.*

The words or groups of words in italics are all *noun phrases* and in these examples they act as subject or object of the main verb 'cooked'. You can move these noun phrases around.

❱ *A delicious supper using leftovers* was waiting on the table when I arrived home.

This noun phrase has moved from being the object to the subject of the sentence.

A *compound sentence* consists of at least two simple sentences joined together by the coordinating conjunctions 'and', 'but' or 'or'.

John	cooked	the supper	and	we	watched	a film
I	I	I	I	I	I	I
Subject	Verb	Object	Conjunction	Subject	Verb	Object

Here 'John cooked the supper' and 'we watched a film' are both simple sentences that can stand alone. We can also add more information while keeping the compound sentence structure:

❯ *Rose's partner, John,* cooked *a delicious supper using leftovers and we all* watched *a really scary film together.*

Complex sentences

A complex sentence contains subordinate clauses, which are added to the main clause but would not stand alone.

To go back to the sentence used earlier: John cooked *a delicious supper using leftovers*. This is a complete, grammatically correct sentence but more can be added to it through the use of *subordinate clauses*. These add extra information but they cannot stand alone.

❯ John cooked a delicious supper using leftovers, *although he usually buys ready meals* (*concession*)

❯ John cooked a delicious supper using leftovers *because he had no time to go shopping* (*reason*)

❯ John cooked a delicious supper using leftovers *when his brother dropped in unexpectedly* (*time*)

❯ John cooked a delicious supper using leftovers, *which we ate in front of the television* (*relative clause*)

There are several areas of sentence grammar that have not been covered in this chapter. When you feel confident with the basics, you can then analyse more complex areas of language use with the help of a good grammar reference book – see some recommendations at the end of this chapter.

For example, you should look at conditionals, reported speech, relative clauses, use of articles and determiners.

Teasers

Here are some questions for you to research the answers to:

❯ When do we use the present perfect tense? (For example, 'I have done ...')

❯ What is the difference between 'mustn't' and 'don't have to'?

❯ What is the difference between 'much' and 'many'?

❯ Why do we say 'bigger' but then 'more comfortable'?

❯ Why do we say 'absolutely boiling' but not 'absolutely hot'?

❯ What is the passive voice? How is it formed? Why is it used?

TEXT LEVEL

Especially in writing, sentences are not usually used in isolation except for functions such as warnings, requests or instructions – for example, 'Do not lean out of the window.' Sentences are usually part of a longer text. If the text is to communicate coherent meaning the sentences need to be in a logical order and should maintain the same degree of formality or informality (*register*).

There will also be language links between some of the sentences to provide cohesion. This can done through the following.

❱ **Repetition** of words or structures.

❱ **Grammatical cohesion:** For example, in a narrative the main verbs should relate to the past; the definite article 'the' is used to link to something already mentioned.

❱ **Lexical cohesion** using synonyms or antonyms, repeating words or using words from the same lexical set. For example, 'Tom got into the car, put the key in the ignition and drove away before he realised he had a flat tyre.' The words underlined all belong to the same lexical set, i.e. they all relate to the topic of cars.

❱ **Referencing:** We use pronouns to connect with something previously mentioned. In the sentence about Tom in the previous paragraph, 'he' is used twice to avoid saying Tom again. Some other pronouns we use in this way are *it, she, they, you, we, this, that, those* and *these*. We can also use adverbs like *there, here, then*. Or the determiner *the*. It is an important reading skill to be able to follow referencing in a text.

❱ **Ellipsis:** Where a word or phrase is missed out because it has already been used, for example 'When I was asked if I could join the meeting, I said I could.' It is not necessary to repeat 'join the meeting'.

❱ **Discourse markers:** These tell the reader what is coming next and how it relates to what has already been said, for example *on the other hand, in conclusion* and *to summarise*.

❱ **Using conjunctions or linkers:** In a narrative we use adverbial linkers such as *next, before, after that,* and *then*. We can also use coordinating conjunctions like *and* (addition), *but* (contrast), *so* (result) and *or* (alternative).

 ## TASK 5.11

Put the following conjunctions/linkers in the table under their basic function. The first one has been done for you.

nevertheless, otherwise, however, furthermore, therefore, moreover, although, hence, also, alternatively, in addition

and	but	so	or
	nevertheless		

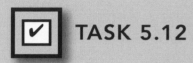

TASK 5.12

Read the following text and answer the questions:

Almost 70 % of air passengers think planes should have child-free zones according to a recent survey. The survey also found that that 35 % would be happy to pay extra on a no-child flight. **Those** on long haul flights would be prepared to pay another £63 for a return ticket on **such** a flight.

1. Can you find a lexical set?

2. What does '**Those**' refer back to?

3. What does '**such**' refer back to?

4. Can you find an example of ellipsis?

5. Can you find an example of the article 'the' used for cohesion?

6. Can you find an example of repetition of a structure?

Spoken grammar/discourse

The examples used in the previous section were mainly given with written English in mind. Spoken language can be very similar, especially in a formal situation or where a speech has been prepared. However, in normal conversation there are differences that a learner should be aware of – learners often begin to write as they speak but there are a number of features of the spoken language that may not be appropriate in writing, for example:

❭ The use of vague words when we can't think of a word – *stuff, thing*

❭ Ellipsis – when a key word is missed out, for example 'Don't know', 'Want to come with us?'

❭ Simpler lexis – *nice, get, ok, and, but*

❭ Simple sentences

❭ The use of fillers – *um, er, like*

There are also features of conversation that ESOL learners my find difficult for two reasons: they may not know the language used or conventions may be different where they have come from.

❭ The use of set phrases or chunks of language – 'How are you?', 'Nice to meet you'.

❭ Set responses, for example: 'Thank you.' 'You're welcome.'; 'I'm sorry.' 'Don't worry about it.'

❭ Discourse markers that are more common in speech: *By the way, obviously, apparently, anyway.*

❯ Turn taking. There are different ways of showing that a turn is finishing and is it therefore not rude for the other person to speak: asking questions, pausing, a fall in intonation.

❯ The use of stress and intonation to convey meaning. For example, we can use stress to show contrast: 'I didn't lose my phone, it was <u>stolen.</u>' Or intonation to show surprise, doubt, and so on.

❯ Showing that you are listening and understanding (back-channelling); for example, 'Really?' and 'How interesting'.

A meaningful conversation is also linked across turns with *cohesive devices* used to connect to what the other person has said:

❯ 'Shall we get a takeaway tonight?'   '<u>That</u>'s a good idea.'

❯ 'I can't find the remote control.'   'When did you last have <u>it</u>?'

PHONOLOGY

The most important consideration when dealing with pronunciation, particularly with ESOL learners, is intelligibility. It is unreasonable to expect learners to sound as if English is their first language – most are happy to retain an accent from the country they come from as are native speakers from the different regions of the UK or other Anglophone countries.

Phonology can be divided into several areas: *sounds* (vowels and consonants), *stress* (sentence and word), *intonation* and the features of *connected speech*. So what are the key elements of each to focus on for intelligibility?

Sounds

Pronunciation of individual phonemes is important. If an ESOL learner mispronounces a word, often they will spell it incorrectly as well.

In terms of spoken intelligibility *long and short vowels* are important. ESOL learners often tend to keep their vowel sounds the same length and this can make them difficult to understand. Look at this phonemic chart for single sound vowels:

/iː/	/ɪ/	/ʊ/	/uː/
seat	sit	good	food
/e/	/ə/	/ɜː/	/ɔː/
head	about	girl	walk
/æ/	/ʌ/	/ɑː/	/ɒ/
had	cup	heart	hot

You will see that the long vowels have the symbol /ː/ after them.

TASK 5.13

Look at the following list of words with single vowels sounds. Which ones have long vowels? Can you match them to the symbol in the chart?

Leave, kit, part, raw, book

Vowel sounds in combination, such as 'road' /əʊ/, which is /ə/ and /ʊ/ run together, are called *diphthongs* and often also cause problems for learners who need to work on lengthening their vowel sounds. The combinations are shown in the chart below:

/ɪə/ year	/eɪ/ they	
/ʊə/ pure	/ɔɪ/ boy	/əʊ/ joke
/eə/ chair	/aɪ/ thigh	/aʊ/ loud

 TASK 5.14

Match these words with the diphthongs in the chart:

here, paid, toy, strive, now

Key consonant sounds can also be an issue for intelligibility, for example if a learner says 'p' instead of 'b', 'back' can sound like 'pack'.

/p/	/b/	/t/	/d/	/tʃ/	/dʒ/	/k/	/g/
pen	bad	ten	day	chip	June	kite	goal
/f/	/v/	/θ/	/ð/	/s/	/z/	/ʃ/	/ʒ/
fine	van	thin	then	sip	zip	ship	leisure
/M/	/N/	/Ŋ/	/H/	/l/	/r/	/w/	/j/
man	now	thing	hat	light	red	wet	yes

Learners often have difficulty with clusters of consonants especially at the ends of words, for example *post* and *clothes*.

Stress

Research has shown that *word stress* is very important. This applies to the fact that in most words one of the syllables is stressed more strongly than the others, for example *dict*ionary, *furn*iture. In fact in two or three syllable words, the stress is usually on the first syllable. More examples are: *luck*y, *beaut*iful and *foll*ow.

However, some two-syllable verbs can be different. Look at the following verbs. Each has the stress on the second syllable.

❱ Decide

❱ Pretend

❱ Accept

❱ Liaise

Some verbs can also be nouns and the stressed syllable shifts: pre*sent* (verb), *pres*ent (noun), re*cord* (verb), *rec*ord (noun). There are several others – say the following words to yourself as verbs and then nouns: object, convict.

While there are some generalised rules for word stress in English, there are many exceptions and it is important to point out the stressed syllable when teaching a new word.

Features of connected speech

So far we have been looking at the pronunciation of individual words. It is important to note that some of these sounds change when words are put together in speech. This is called *connected speech*. This is important for natural sounding speech but it can make it difficult for ESOL learners to understand fluent speakers as they may not hear some of the words and they may not be able to identify where one word ends and another begins (word boundaries). It is important to teach learners to speak as naturally as possible so that they can understand others and be understood.

One key feature of connected speech is *linking* – where a word beginning with a vowel 'borrows' the consonant from the end of the previous word, for example 'can ni ha va napple?'

On other occasions, sounds may change (*assimilation*): 'handbag' becomes 'hambag'.

Extra sounds can appear (*intrusion*): 'You need to see ya doctor'.

Also, sounds can disappear altogether (*elision*): when we say 'fish and chips' we elide the last sound in 'and' (/d/) and say 'fish /ən/ chips' rather than 'fish /ənd/ chips'.

Another key feature of spoken English is that vowels in unstressed words can change to /ə/, known as the schwa or weak form. For example, in 'I can swim', 'can' is unstressed and so is pronounced /cən/ rather than /cæn/

 TASK 5.15

Read the following sentence aloud.

At ten to two, I left the house to meet a friend at the station but the train was early and my friend had already got a taxi.

Now, try and identify where the weak form of the vowel is used.

Sounds and symbols

In English, unlike many other languages, there is not always a straightforward relationship between sounds and written symbols.

Some sounds can be represented in different ways in writing: for example, *fair, rare, mayor, bear, layer, their, there* and *they're* are all **/eə/**.

Some words are spelled differently, and have different meanings, even though they sound the same. These are known as *homophones* and can cause great difficulty for literacy learners: *their, there* and *they're* are good examples.

Some groups of letters are pronounced differently depending on the word: for example, *enough, bough, trough, though* and *thought*. This means that learners can't always read or spell a word through sounding it out. They may need to use other strategies.

The language features discussed in this chapter are not usually taught in isolation but are integrated within a lesson focusing on a particular topic or context, such as applying for a job or health. Such a lesson will include some or all of the four skills of reading, writing, speaking and listening which are discussed in the next chapter and will provide opportunities for encountering, practising and revising language.

FURTHER READING

Albery, D. (2012) *The TKT Course: Knowledge About Language*. Cambridge: Cambridge University Press.

Crystal, D. (1988) *Rediscover Grammar*. London: Longman.

Hancock, M. (2003) *English Pronunciation in Use*. Cambridge: Cambridge University Press.

Lewis, M. (2002*) Implementing the Lexical Approach: Putting theory into Practice*. Boston, MA: Thomson Heinle.

Parrott, M. (2010) *Grammar for English Language Teachers*. Cambridge: Cambridge University Press.

Thornbury, S. (1997) About Language: Tasks for Teachers of English. Cambridge: Cambridge University Press.

Thornbury, S. (2005) *Beyond the Sentence: Introducing Discourse Analysis*. London: Macmillan.

Thorne, S. (2008) *Mastering Advanced English Language*. London: Palgrave.

6 The four skills: Speaking, listening, reading, writing

Irene Schwab

INTRODUCTION

Where literacy learners are focused on learning skills, ESOL learners generally put more emphasis on learning language. However, skills are also important for language learners. For example, although an ESOL learner might be a fluent writer in their own language, they may be unused to the genres, the types of discourse and the conventions of writing in English. So teachers of both ESOL and literacy need to focus on all four skills of reading, writing, speaking and listening.

We are all aware that if someone comes to a country where they don't speak the dominant language, they are likely to have difficulties communicating with residents of that country. But many of us are less conscious of the effects of limited literacy. With so many texts all around us, both online and on paper, it can be hard for people to imagine what it is like to feel uncomfortable with reading and writing. If the newspapers are to be believed, this is all down to problems with spelling and grammar; they argue that if people had learned these at school, everyone would be able to read and write perfectly. In this chapter we look in detail at the four skills that we use to carry out literacy practices in the twenty-first century, and see that there is much more to communication than spelling and grammar. In fact, as we can see from the ubiquity of texting as a form of mass communication, accurate spelling and grammar may not be necessary at all in some circumstances.

While we would all like to be comfortable in all four of the language skills, most of us are more comfortable with some than with others. For example, teachers often fall into the trap of talking with a great deal of facility in lessons and might be surprised when an observer notes that they didn't listen to their learners as much as they might have; a professional counsellor might be an active and intense listener but still find it hard to write academic papers about their subject; an academic who continuously reads challenging academic literature and adds to it with her own papers may still quake at the idea of talking about her subject in public lectures.

 TASK 6.1

Below are three cases where someone might feel uncomfortable in one or more of the four skills. Why might these be difficult? Jot down any ideas you have.

❱ Making a speech at a wedding

❱ Writing a condolence letter

❱ Reading a legal document

Detailed answers are given on p. 117 but an overarching reason why these might be difficult is that they are all literacy practices that we do not take part in on a daily basis. We may feel confident in our everyday discourses, but put in a situation where the practices are different, we can feel outside our comfort zone. What we need here is to have an awareness of *the discourse that is associated with particular practices*. One aspect of this is *register*. This is the way that language changes according to the context in which it is used. Getting the register right can be difficult, especially when the culture of the person/people you are speaking to is different from your own and alternative rules might apply. One of the issues is that the 'rules' are not written down; they are just 'understood' or *tacit*.

So we can see that spelling and grammar are certainly not the only issues around the four skills; there are many other factors that can cause problems for the person trying to communicate. In the following sections we will consider a number of issues that might make one or more of the four skills difficult for even fluent and experienced users of English and explore some pedagogical options for the language and literacy teacher.

READING

Reading and understanding a text depends on three key elements:

❱ The **task/purpose** for reading and what this implies

❱ The **reader** (and the skills, strategies and motivation s/he brings)

❱ The **text** and its language and structure

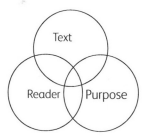

So increasing the reader's skill at reading is only part of the challenge. As well as helping learners develop their skills, teachers also have to provide them with strategies: to help them be clear about their purposes for reading and the different ways of reading that each purpose implies and to help them deal with 'inconsiderate texts' (ones that are not written clearly or simply).

PURPOSE

We read for many different purposes and this will involve approaching texts in a variety of different ways. Think for example of:

❱ an advert on a billboard

❱ the newspaper

❱ Facebook to catch up with your friends' activities

❯ a text on your mobile phone

❯ a novel

❯ an election leaflet that is slipped under your door

❯ a text book for study

❯ a blog

❯ health and safety instructions at work

You will read each of these in different ways depending on your purpose for reading. You might flick quickly through the newspaper to get an idea of what is going on today (*skim reading*) or you might glance at Facebook to see if any of your friends have posted something new (*scanning* for new information). Others, like the novel, you will read quite carefully, although you might skip the boring bits. Reading the textbook might involve you in very detailed reading (although probably only in relevant sections) and, perhaps, also *note-taking*, so you remember the important bits. The election leaflet will involve yet another type of reading – *critical reading* – where you analyse the text to find out how far to believe what is being claimed.

So we can see we have at least four types of reading:

❯ **Skimming:** Reading a text quickly to get the gist.

❯ **Scanning:** Reading a text quickly to find a particular piece of information.

❯ **Reading for detail:** The amount of detail will depend on the task, for example reading a novel will be different from reading a text book.

❯ **Critical reading:** Reading between the lines to find out what the writer is *really* saying.

We cannot just teach one type of reading but must help learners to become familiar with different types of texts and strategies for approaching each.

	Skimming	Scanning	Reading for detail	Critical reading
What skills does it involve?	Using headings, subheadings and images to give clues	Focusing on key words or numbers to find what you want and ignoring irrelevant information	Selecting what is relevant and picking out key points	Trying to see what the author is saying by his/her choice of words and images and how they are organised on the page or screen

Reading critically

We can sometimes forget that every text has an author and that this person has both a reason for writing and an audience in mind. When we read an advertisement, we can usually tell that we are being persuaded to buy or do something. However, in other texts it might not be so easy to recognise what the writer has in mind. For example, articles in different newspapers might be aimed at very different audiences; the blurb on the back of a novel, or indeed on a packet of cereal, is not just neutral information but designed to make you want to buy the item; the writer of a blog on the Internet may also have a particular axe to grind. So helping learners to read between the lines, to identify fact and fiction, and to recognise bias are all important aspects of reading in the twenty-first century.

THE READER

One of the key issues in understanding a text is the amount of prior knowledge that the reader brings to it. For example look at the following headline and first sentence from an article on the BBC website and consider what it is about, and how prior knowledge might help you read it.

Celtic v Barcelona: Champions League 'revenge' not driving Barca

Barcelona insist revenge is not their motivation when they visit Celtic in the Champions League on Tuesday. The Hoops caused one of the major European shocks last season when they beat the Catalans 2–1 in the group stages at Celtic Park.

Barcelona will be without World Player of the Year Lionel Messi this time.

http://www.bbc.co.uk/sport/0/football/24330753

You probably guessed that it was about *football*, but that word is never used. So how did you know? You might have used a *lexical set* – words that together are used in particular contexts, so for example here: *Champions League, player, beat*. Of course, they may indicate another sport, but prior knowledge again would help you place *Barcelona* and *Celtic* as football teams and *Lionel Messi* as a famous player. Even if you got this far, the *Hoops* and the *Catalans* might still fox you without more detailed knowledge (in football jargon, horizontal stripes such as those on Celtic's shirts, are called 'hoops'; Barcelona is a Catalan city with a renowned football team).

So, the more you know beforehand, the easier the text will be to read and understand. We call this a *schema*, a mental picture that one has of a particular topic or idea. If you can draw on (*activate*) whatever you know already about a topic, you can add the new knowledge to this and construct a clearer picture.

The reader can do other things to enhance their reading of unfamiliar texts: they can develop their vocabulary and they can develop their fluency in reading.

Developing vocabulary

It is said that in order to read comfortably, a reader needs to know 98 per cent of the words in a text. A literacy learner may know the words but not be able to recognise them in print; an ESOL learner may not know the words at all. For many struggling readers it is a combination of both. Research shows that extensive reading develops vocabulary and having a large vocabulary helps one to read more easily. In other words, the two are inextricably linked. Understanding words is a continuum, from no knowledge at all to complete knowledge. It might be illustrated in a diagram:

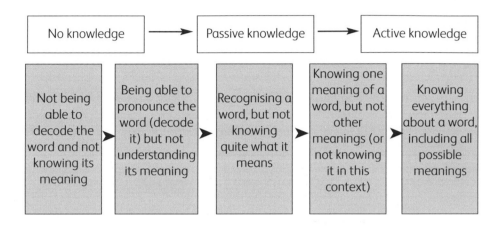

How can a teacher help learners develop their vocabulary? Of course, learning to use a dictionary is important, but another key strategy is teaching groups of words rather than single words in isolation.

❱ Activate learners' *schemata* (plural of schema) before reading so that learners can pool the knowledge they have between them (for example, some learners will know about football; others current affairs). Learners can explain words they know to each other.

❱ Build *lexical sets* of words and phrases, maybe through a *graphic organiser* such as a mind map (for example, football verbs such as *kick, score, tackle*; nouns such as *foul, goal, referee*, and so on).

❱ Explore word origins (for example through prefixes and suffixes such as knowing that *dis-* makes a word into its opposite (obey–disobey; placed–displaced); or that *-able* turns a verb into an adjective (agree–agreeable; love–lovable).

However you choose to introduce vocabulary, make sure that learners have *multiple exposure* to the new words (repeated introduction in different contexts) and that they *engage actively* with the new words (use them in speech and writing). Choose words to work on that have meaning for learners and they will have more motivation to learn and use them:

❱ Key words for their interests – home, leisure, work use (nouns and verbs)

❱ Words that are used frequently in reading and writing (for example the Dolch list of the one hundred most common words)

❱ Words that are needed to 'glue' texts together (prepositions, adverbs, pronouns)

Developing fluency

Fluency is a combination of speed and accuracy in recognising and decoding words. Developing fluency means working on a small part of a text, practising reading it individually, in pairs or in a group until the reader can read it with expression, speed and accuracy. Research has shown that fluency in reading supports comprehension of the text.

THE TEXT

There is little the reader can do about difficult texts apart from devise strategies to handle them. The teacher can, of course, simplify any text, which will be useful for classroom practice, but in the long run the aim is for learners to be able to read any text they come across. There are a number of strategies that have been shown to aid understanding of texts, many of them assisting the learner in checking their own understanding of the text as they read. A combination of these techniques is likely to be even more effective.

Comprehension strategies

- **Comprehension monitoring**: Checking one's understanding as one goes along.
- **Graphic organisers:** Using tables, charts and mind maps to record information in visual ways.
- **Story structure:** Understanding how stories are structured, i.e. with a beginning, middle and end.
- **Question answering**: Answering different types of questions to explore facets of the text.
- **Question generating:** Even better is generating one's own questions to be answered by the text.
- **Summarisation:** Making a summary of what one has read.
- **Multiple strategies:** Using more than one of these at the same time.

Reciprocal reading

In this activity multiple strategies are used to support and develop text comprehension. Learners read a text collaboratively, taking specific roles within the group, each contributing towards creating meaning. One predicts what will happen in the next section to be read (using clues in the text and prior knowledge of the topic); one clarifies anything that is unclear; one asks questions to be answered by reading on; one summarises what has been read. The roles can stay the same or change. In this way, learners can work together to create meaning, initially supported by the teacher, but with her gradually withdrawing, allowing them to monitor their reading themselves.

WRITING

Writing is, perhaps, the skill that has changed most in recent years. Whereas thirty years ago, it might have been letters, notes and memos that we employed to communicate with colleagues, friends and family, now we mostly use texts, tweets and emails. However, research shows that we do not, as some think, rely on shortened forms such as *u* or *l8* as much as people think. Despite a decrease in formality in what we write, most people still write in sentences.

One of the things that tends to stop us writing is that we are concerned about making mistakes. Texting is fine because we are not expected to write in formal sentences or use conventional spelling. But for other types of writing, even though we have generally become more informal, we still expect to be judged according to the 'correctness' of our writing. However, writing can be technically correct but not very readable. Chomsky's famous sentence, 'Colorless green ideas sleep furiously' is an example of a sentence that is grammatical but makes no sense. Usually, even with errors of spelling, punctuation or grammar, we can get the message. It only becomes a problem if the writing loses clarity and the writer is unable to communicate in the form they are trying to use. So, an effective writer is someone who is able to express what they want to say, in the format they are trying to use (which may be a conventional one), to communicate with the intended audience.

These are the key issues in developing learners' writing skills; a good writer makes choices based on their ability to integrate these elements. Learners will come with a purpose for writing; they may be able to focus on their audience but they might need help to pick an appropriate format to meet their needs. One problem faced by many beginning and developing writers is that they write as they speak. It can be helpful for them to learn that there are certain conventions that we use which make expression in writing very different from speaking.

Genre

Different formats are used for different purposes and they involve the use of appropriate language, structure and layout. The language, structure and layout together form the *genre* of formal letters and if you are able to learn the genres that you might want to use, it will put you in a more powerful position, alongside those people who can use them easily and effectively. For example a letter, an academic report or a menu would be immediately recognisable to someone who had seen such texts before. By studying the features of each text type, a reader can become familiar with the language and structure that is typically used and, by knowing what to expect, the writing will be made easier.

TASK 6.2

Consider a formal letter and make some notes on what you might need to know about each of these three elements:

❯ Language

❯ Structure

❯ Layout

Genres have changed over time and continue to change (as we have seen, the trend is to become more informal) and they vary across cultures so ESOL learners and older literacy learners may have to relearn genres that they can use adeptly in their own language or language variety. Understanding genres can be quite complex. Sometimes they might seem superficially similar but contain key differences.

 TASK 6.3

What might be the differences in genre between these writing tasks?

》 An email to your child away at university

》 An email to a work colleague

》 An email to the council about council tax

Teaching writing skills involves supporting the learner to build confidence in their own voice to express what they want to say in the format they choose to use. The teacher can help learners understand genres by:

》 showing examples of typical genres and analysing together their language, structure and layout;

》 modelling how the genres work by demonstrating the process of writing. The teacher might discuss why she makes the choices she does in writing a piece of her own;

》 using tools such as writing frames which *scaffold* the process so that learners do not have to concentrate on all aspects of writing at the same time; and

》 setting writing tasks in which learners can work together, discussing the process and making decisions collaboratively – again a way of scaffolding writing.

As we have seen above, in order to reproduce a recognisable text type the writer needs to ensure that the language, structure and layout will be recognised by readers as appropriate for that genre. Even experienced writers find it hard to construct a piece of writing they are happy with first time round. One thing teachers can do is to share details of how difficult it is even for expert writers to 'get it right' without drafting and redrafting, and reassure learners that this is not 'cheating' but a useful strategy.

The process approach

One way of doing this is to introduce the *process approach* to writing. This helps learners to see the process of writing as one in which the writer is not expected to get it right immediately they put pen to paper (or the electronic equivalent). Instead it is an iterative process with a series of distinct stages:

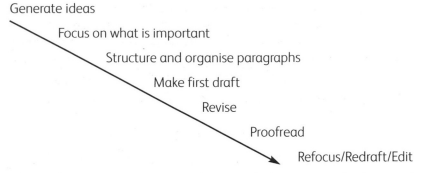

Generate ideas

    Focus on what is important

        Structure and organise paragraphs

           Make first draft

             Revise

               Proofread

                 Refocus/Redraft/Edit

This is often represented as a cycle in which the process of refocusing/redrafting and editing can lead back to generating more ideas and another draft. In practice, this is how many writers hone their texts and control their writing to make it fit its purpose.

Again, it can be helpful for the teacher to model such a process to show how at each stage the different choices add to the development and control of the written text. The use of word processing packages can be very helpful in making the redrafting process less cumbersome.

There are particular difficulties that face the writer who is learning to write in a different language from their mother tongue:

> The genres used in the UK may be very different from those they are used to.

> They may not be familiar with grammatical forms they need to use.

> They may not know items of vocabulary they wish to use.

> There may be letter or sound combinations that are unfamiliar in their own language, which make spelling difficult.

> They may not be familiar with the Roman script.

> Punctuation conventions may be different in their own script.

> They may not be familiar with writing at all – either because their language is not written down or because they did not have the opportunity to have an education in their own country.

Audience

Developing a sense of audience is an important part of being able to communicate what is intended in the way that will have the most impact. The concept of critical literacy is also important for the new writer and affects the choices he makes. Choosing the right degree of formality, intimacy and politeness involves an understanding of the nuances of different types of discourse. It also necessitates an understanding of how language can be used to have particular effects on the reader: for example, the choice of vocabulary ('What word should I use: slim, slender, thin, skinny?') and grammatical constructions (consider the difference an active or passive form makes to exposing or hiding agency of an action). An ESOL learner working on particular functions in English will need to learn how to express these in writing as well as in speech.

TASK 6.4

What audience are these email invitations to dinner aimed at? Can you put them in order of familiarity with the audience?

1. I'd like to ask if you would come for dinner next week

2. Would you like to go out for dinner some time?

3. May we have the honour of your presence at dinner on 15 May?

4. Fancy dinner?

Spelling, punctuation and grammar

In addition to decisions about the level of formality to be used, the writer also has choices about the degree to which Standard English is necessary and the level of accuracy required in terms of spelling, punctuation and grammar. Although Standard English is the most prestigious variety of English and is important for formal communications, its use might be inappropriate in certain types of writing (texts or emails to friends, diary entries, poetry) where people might feel they can express themselves more comfortably or more creatively in their own variety of English.

As we have seen above, the conventions around writing are changing all the time and the trend is towards more informality. Complete accuracy in writing is difficult to achieve for the new writer and, again, not always necessary. It is useful to discuss with beginner writers how much their intended audience will be concerned about correct spelling, punctuation and grammar as long as the message comes across clearly and coherently.

However, spelling, punctuation and grammar are also the areas of writing that learners often worry about most because they are seen as the most evident signs of 'being literate' and teachers often share their learners' concerns. Spelling and punctuation do not exist in speech; they only occur in writing and therefore they should largely be taught within the context of writing rather than in isolation. The teaching of grammar has been discussed in detail in Chapter 5.

For spelling work, it is best to work on words that arise from meaningful contexts. These might be:

❭ the learner's own writing;

❭ a text the learner has read; or

❭ key words that the learner might want to use at some point (names, addresses, words relating to their work or leisure activities).

There are a number of different ways to work on spelling. These include:

❭ strategies based around understanding word structure, such as common prefixes and suffixes (like plurals);

❭ strategies based on phonics (understanding common sound–symbol patterns);

❭ strategies for memorising unusual spellings, such as mnemonics, sounding out words, Look, Say, Cover, Write, Check; and

❭ rules (but remember exceptions).

Punctuation is also impossible to learn in isolation from writing. In the *Adult Literacy Core Curriculum* it is situated as part of sentence focus work. This is because an understanding of how to use punctuation is inextricable from knowledge of how a sentence works. For example, in order to learn where to put a full stop or a comma, or understand capitalisation of the first word of a sentence, learners need to recognise what a sentence is and the different ways in which it can be constructed.

New writers can feel uncomfortable and apprehensive when writing because it has a permanence that exposes one's errors and uncertainties. Teachers can help to reduce anxiety about writing by:

❭ providing low-stakes tasks (ones that are not of great importance);

❭ giving opportunities for collaborative writing;

❭ scaffolding writing by using tools such as writing frames or word banks (for spellings);

❭ encouraging the use of computer spell-checking, translation tools or dictionaries;

❭ supplying model texts as examples; and

❭ scribing for learners.

SPEAKING

Many people learn a language in school only to find that when they visit a country where it is spoken, they are unable to communicate, even when they know the words. It is difficult to maintain both fluency and accuracy in a new language. However, there is sometimes an assumption that if English is one's native language, speaking should be no problem. Even for those people born to English-speaking families, there are still occasions where we might feel tongue-tied or nervous about approaching certain speaking tasks, as we saw above in making a speech.

In order to speak with clarity and confidence we need:

❭ to know the language well enough – discourse, grammar and vocabulary;

❭ to be clear about our audience and how to address them (correct register, appropriate choice of language and vocabulary);

❭ to understand the format/genre/function of what we are trying to say (this will affect the language, length of speech, structure and type of utterance); and

❭ to be confident in what we are saying – which involves all the above together with experience in that type of discourse.

One difference between literacy and ESOL learners is that while literacy learners are probably speaking in English for much, if not all, of their time outside the classroom, ESOL learners may use very little English beyond the classroom. So, learners need plenty of practice speaking in class, both for its own sake and because research shows that talk also helps develop the other three language skills.

For literacy learners

Learners already know how to talk in everyday situations but might need help to develop confidence, structure and coherence when speaking in more formal contexts such as interviews or making presentations.

Research has shown that focused discussion in a literacy class prepares learners better for reading and writing tasks.

For ESOL learners

The teacher's language is a model and learners will learn from listening to the teacher talk as long as it is graded appropriately. The teacher needs to be using predominantly language the learner already knows, but she will intermittently introduce new examples of language use.

However, the more you talk, the less opportunity there is for the learners to talk, so you need to strictly control the amount of 'teacher talk'. Remember talk is work in the ESOL classroom.

You need to encourage the learners to talk both in controlled situations (working on a particular function like asking questions) and informally (working on a task together and talking in order to complete it: for example, a collaborative, problem-solving task).

 TASK 6.5

Here are some tasks that you might set to develop speaking skills.

❭ Discussion

❭ Role play

❭ Prepared presentation

❭ Communication games and tasks

❭ Drilling and controlled practice

Think about when and why you might use the activities and then answer these questions for each one.

>) Is it suitable for literacy, ESOL or both?
>
>) Does it practise speaking, listening or both?
>
>) What is it useful for?

As part of developing their speaking skills ESOL learners also need to learn about pronunciation (stress, intonation and features of connected speech) (see Chapter 5).

LISTENING

We tend to think of speaking and listening as going together and, of course, in many cases they do. However, there are often occasions when you might listen without taking part in a conversation, for example, listening to a TV or radio programme, a film or YouTube clip, or the lyrics of a song. This is why at a rough estimate, we are said to spend about 45 per cent of our communication time in listening (the other skills lag behind: 9 per cent writing, 16 per cent reading, 30 per cent speaking).

Nevertheless, listening frequently integrates with the other skills; for example, when chatting, we are listening as well as speaking; or we might listen to an answerphone message and write a note of its contents.

In some cases we will have *paralinguistic devices* to assist us with our listening. These include facial expressions, hand gestures, and how we hold and use our body. But sometimes the only clue to meaning that we can get is through listening. Our purpose for listening can vary depending on the situation.

 TASK 6.6

Think about the listening experiences below.

>) Your doctor is giving you the result of some tests
>
>) Weather forecast on the radio
>
>) Someone giving you directions
>
>) Chatting to a neighbour in the street

For each one try to answer the following questions:

>) What is the purpose of the listening (what are you listening for)?
>
>) What might be difficult about it?
>
>) Do you need to speak as well as listen?

Most of us find it is quite hard to concentrate on listening for a long period of time so we have the ability to 'switch off' and let the sounds wash over us. We only tune in and listen when we have a purpose for doing so and our purpose will determine how we go about listening. So when you give a listening task to learners, they need to have a clear purpose so they know *how* they are meant to be listening.

For example, in the task above, you might have noted that in listening to the weather forecast, your purpose might be to find out what the weather will be like in your area the next day. If you live in London, you don't need to listen in detail to the forecast for the north or the west of the country. So a teacher setting a task on listening to the weather forecast needs to alert learners that they will be listening for certain words/phrases and they can ignore the rest. However, just listen for the word London and you might still miss what you want to hear.

What other key words might the learner be listening out for? There might be various options:

❯ The capital

❯ The south or the south-east

❯ The Home Counties

❯ The southern part of the country

In the case of the weather forecast, the details are important. When is the rain likely to start? Will it be cold enough to need a coat? However, sometimes we don't need to worry about detail, we just need to get the general idea. This is called listening for *gist*.

TASK 6.7

Think about these listening tasks. Does the learner need to listen for gist or details? If details, what are they?

❯ Watching a sitcom on TV

❯ A friend telling a joke

❯ The answerphone message when you ring an office

❯ A lecture at college

Some people are better at listening for gist; others at getting detail. There are some occasions where you have to listen in detail to a large amount of information all at once (like an important lecture or taking complicated directions) which is akin to reading for detail, but without the option of going back and checking. The skill of note-taking might accompany listening here and people often find writing while listening particularly challenging. Another thing to bear in mind with listening is that all sorts of things can make it more difficult, for example a speaker who talks too fast or with an unfamiliar accent, bad acoustics in the room or noise interference.

Developing listening skills

Listening tasks need to be carefully structured. In real life we may just listen idly (the couple behind you on the bus) but usually we listen deliberately and with a clear purpose. The teacher needs to set up a task so that it feels authentic to the learners. They also need to be clear what they are doing and why and what they will be learning from it.

A good listening activity:

⟩ has a clear purpose

⟩ requires the learner to listen according to that purpose

⟩ doesn't require the learner to write or read at the same time (or only minimally)

⟩ is staged with tasks before, during and after listening

In pre-listening tasks, the teacher might:

⟩ generate interest in the topic

⟩ encourage learners to share what they already know about the topic

⟩ discuss words/grammar points/textual features that learners might find difficult

While listening, the teacher might choose *one* of these tasks:

⟩ A task that involves learners listening for the gist

⟩ A task that involves learners listening for the key points

⟩ A task that involves learners listening for a significant detail

⟩ A task that involves learners listening for several different details

She will need to play the recording or repeat the text more than once, perhaps stopping at various points to ask questions or give prompts.

In post-listening tasks, the teacher might:

⟩ check listeners' achievement of the task by asking questions/monitoring their work;

⟩ go over the task, replaying the recording and stopping it at various points to discuss aspects of the language/content;

⟩ pick up on particular language points to discuss further; and

⟩ pick up on various content points to encourage discussion or writing activities.

INTEGRATING THE FOUR SKILLS

We started this chapter looking at each skill in turn, but in practice we rarely separate them out like this.

Many learners have *spiky profiles*; that is, they are better at some skills than others. For example, most literacy learners find reading easier than writing. ESOL learners who have not had much education, but who have been in the country for some time, might find speaking and listening easier than reading and writing. Other ESOL learners who are highly educated in their own country might be used to reading and writing in English but have little experience of informal speaking and listening.

Spelling, punctuation and grammar

Knowledge of grammar plays a part in all four skills, as a clue to meaning in reading and listening; in accurately conveying meaning in writing and speaking. Spelling and punctuation can also be important in writing, where they help a writer to communicate clearly and coherently, but they are not the only, or even necessarily the most important, factor in clear and coherent writing.

 TASK 6.8

Most communicative activities entail the use of more than one skill. Think about what skills might be involved in:

❭ helping a child with her homework

❭ talking to the doctor

❭ travelling somewhere new on the bus

❭ checking your Facebook page

Setting authentic tasks will enable learners to practise all four skills in the types of tasks they will be required to do in real life. Where these are collaborative tasks, this also enables them both to work on their stronger skills, thus building confidence and motivation, and to have more practice in those skills they need to develop with the support of someone who is more proficient in that skill. Collaborative projects might be role plays, research projects, problem-solving tasks and so on.

Tasks that involve the use of technology may be more motivating for some learners who are used to technology playing a central role in their lives. However, it may not be the case for others, who might find new technology frightening and unfamiliar. If you have both types of learner in a class, you might need either to gradually introduce technology into the lessons with the support of other learners, or to differentiate so that tasks can be done with or without computers or mobile technology.

FURTHER READING

Duncan, S. (2012) *Reading Circles, Novels and Adult Reading Development*. London: Continuum.

Hughes, N. and Schwab, I. (2010) *Teaching Adult Literacy: Principles and Practice*. Maidenhead: Open University Press.

NRDC (2007) *Developing Adult Teaching and Learning: Practitioner Guides*. Leicester: NIACE.

- Burton, M., *Reading*

- Cooke, M. and Roberts, C., *ESOL*

- Grief, S., *Writing*

Paton, A. and Wilkins, M. (2009) *Teaching Adult ESOL: Principles and Practice*. Maidenhead: Open University Press.

Sunderland, H. and Spiegel, M. (2006) *Teaching Basic Literacy to ESOL Learners*. London: LLU+.

7 Planning learning for inclusive practice

Irene Schwab

INTRODUCTION

This chapter deals with two important questions for literacy and ESOL teachers:

⟩ How do you design a course, and individual lessons, that will help the learners acquire the skills and language they need to engage in their chosen practices?

⟩ How do you ensure that the curriculum you design is interesting, relevant and accessible for all the learners in the group?

The word 'curriculum' is often used interchangeably with course, syllabus or scheme of work. However, strictly speaking they all have slightly different meanings.

⟩ A *curriculum* is formed through a set of beliefs or theories, which may be entrenched in a set of official standards, for example the national curriculum for schools.

⟩ A *syllabus* is a practical way of representing that curriculum, by outlining how those theories or standards might be covered in a programme of study (i.e. a *course*).

⟩ The actual programme of work devised by the team to suit the learners and to fit the time and staffing available would be called the *scheme of work*.

In terms of a literacy or ESOL course:

⟩ The *curriculum* is based on a set of national standards, stating what a learner should be able to do at each level. There is a different national core curriculum for adult literacy and for ESOL, but these are based on a shared set of standards.

⟩ A qualification is based on a *syllabus* designed by an awarding body (for example, City and Guilds or AQA). The syllabus states what has to be covered to gain the qualification.

⟩ A *course* is the programme designed to deliver the syllabus. Course books have been designed for some courses (for example, Cambridge First Certificate or GCSE English) but, in general, course books are not available for most literacy and ESOL courses as so much depends on the individual learner's needs and interests.

⟩ A *scheme of work* is developed by the course team, showing the work that will be covered during the learning programme.

PLANNING A LEARNING PROGRAMME

What you decide is an appropriate programme of study may be the result of discussions with learners, colleagues and managers and it will dictate how you plan your course. Of course, not everyone has complete freedom of choice in planning what they teach. Many of us are obliged to follow a curriculum that is set by our organisation or curriculum manager. And even for those lucky enough to have some choices, there are many factors to take into account when thinking about writing a programme.

TASK 7.1

What factors should a teacher be considering when planning a course?

These factors will all impact on what you are able to do when planning a course. Bearing these in mind, you also have to produce a programme of work that is logical, coherent and developmental for the learners and is inclusive so that everyone in the group is able to get the most from it.

We have looked at some of these factors in earlier chapters (see Chapters 2 and 4). When you are planning a course, you need to be considering the balance of a number of different types of professional knowledge:

❭ Teaching the four skills
❭ Teaching language relevant to the learners' level and needs
❭ Teaching different genres/functions
❭ Knowledge of learners' backgrounds, interests and aspirations

Inclusion

The programme that you devise will be for the whole group, but the group is made up of individuals and you are responsible for ensuring that everyone is included in the learning opportunities. In order to have an inclusive curriculum, the contents of the curriculum need to be presented in a staged and balanced manner. The core curriculum will help with the staging and also makes some suggestions for integrating the skills. Staging learning means that it is organised with activities sequenced in a logical way so that learners can move from one activity to another, steadily building their knowledge and skills.

TASK 7.2

If you were teaching about punctuation in writing, which of these would you teach first? Reorder these punctuation marks into the order you would teach them to a literacy class.

❭ Comma
❭ Sentence beginning and ending
❭ Apostrophe
❭ Question mark
❭ Capital letters for proper nouns

The reason that sentence beginning and ending is the first thing to be taught is not because it's the easiest. In fact, understanding what a sentence is can be quite a difficult concept to grasp and one which many fluent writers still struggle with. Additionally, those who learned to write in a language other than English might have quite different concepts of a sentence. But the reason *sentence boundaries* are taught first is that knowledge about punctuation is useless unless it is incorporated into the act of writing and it is hard to write coherently without breaking the text into sentences. Communicating clearly to a reader requires writing that makes use of capital letters and full stops. There is no point considering other types of punctuation until a learner has some sense of what a sentence is (although they may not understand it completely until later).

So, when planning a scheme of work, you need to ensure that it is carefully staged so that the learning that is essential comes first and is then built upon in later sessions. These later sessions will be a mixture of:

❯ Revision of previously learned language/skills

❯ Introduction of new (planned) language/skills

❯ Integration and synthesis of new and old language/skills

❯ Unplanned language/skills that need to be dealt with there and then because they have been noticed by one or more learners and raised as a question

Differentiation

This is made more complex by the fact that you are working with adults who have experience of life and language and every time you introduce something new there will be some learners who know it already, as well as some for whom it is totally new. Additionally, as you practise new structures or skills, some will grasp them more quickly than others. Some people in the group might be ready to move on, while others still need more practice.

There are many other differences between people that will affect how they learn. For example:

❯ **Attention:** Some people find it harder than others to concentrate for long periods.

❯ **Interest:** We all have some things that grip us and others that totally bore us.

❯ **Motivation:** See Chapter 2 for a discussion of intrinsic and extrinsic motivation.

❯ **Cognitive issues:** People have different ways of processing information and memorising it.

❯ **Learning styles:** While we no longer label people as visual, aural and kinaesthetic learners, some people do have preferences for how they like to learn.

❯ **Physical needs:** Some people will need adjustments to the physical environment or the learning resources.

❯ **Psychological needs:** Some learners need more support and reassurance than others.

❯ **World knowledge:** Some people will need more explanations to set the context for their reading or listening tasks.

❱ **Knowledge of and about the English language:** This will affect how well people can perform certain tasks or how much support they will need.

❱ **Previous learning experiences:** This may affect how people prefer (or prefer not) to learn.

So, the teacher planning a course has to take into account not just how she *stages* the learning, but also how she *differentiates* it, so that everyone is included and everyone is helped to develop their skills at their own pace. Differentiation is one of the most difficult roles of the teacher. She needs to organise the learning so that everyone in the group regardless of all the differences between them – physical, sensory, cognitive, social, cultural and motivational – is able to learn something that is relevant to their needs and interests. With this many factors to take into account, some people ask why we don't plan individual learning programmes for everyone in the class? Some teachers do, of course, especially if they have a small group or one that meets infrequently. However, planning and providing activities and materials for every individual learner would take a heavy toll on the teacher's time. In addition, research has shown that collaborative learning offers benefits that cannot be gained through individual study.

Differentiation can take many forms. It can be organised through the content of the lesson (the concepts or skills you are teaching), the process (the activities you employ to teach them) or the product (the outcome of the learning). If you are working with a group, in order to make the class coherent and manageable at least one of these should remain the same for all learners.

If you want the entire group to have the same content, you need to differentiate the process of learning (the activities) or the product of learning (the expected outcome). For example, if the content is to be the NHS and the outcome a written explanation of what the NHS does, reading activities might consist of different subgroups containing items like:

❱ Reading NHS Choices website and reviewing its contents

❱ Reading a newspaper article about a potential local hospital closure

❱ Reading a blog written by someone who works for the NHS

❱ Reading a leaflet outlining what the local health centre offers

The teacher might bring the group together after this and ask learners to tell each other what they had found out, leading to a discussion before the learners all write an explanatory piece.

Or the teacher might decide that she wants to differentiate the outcome so learners might start together by reading the same text or having a discussion, but then work towards different outcomes. For example:

❱ Writing an opinion of the NHS

❱ Giving a presentation about their own experience of English hospitals or doctors

❱ Responding to a posting or an article on the Web

❱ Producing a group project with photos of local health provision and captions

Differentiation by content, process or product

	Content	Process	Product
What to differentiate	What learners need to learn	Ways in which the content is taught	Ways of demonstrating what has been learned
Examples	Concepts and skills	Activities	Outcomes
Methods of differentiation	Vary content according to learner interests	Flexible grouping and variety of activities	Provide options for different outcomes

So, when planning a course, a teacher needs to consider for each session how she will differentiate:

❯ Will the same content motivate all the learners in the group or does it need to be differentiated to accommodate different interests?

❯ Are the same activities appropriate for all members of the group, or should they be differentiated to accommodate different learning preferences and language or literacy levels?

❯ Is it necessary to have the same outcome for all learners or can different ways of practising and demonstrating learning be accommodated?

What sorts of teaching methods differentiate best?

As a literacy or ESOL teacher, you have a huge choice of activities to choose from. Not all of these will suit all groups of learners or individuals. In addition, some will enable you to differentiate better than others. Here are a few examples to consider.

❯ **Graduated worksheets:** Learners can answer questions, fill in gaps, reorder or match up language items. If more than one worksheet is to be completed, they can be graduated in order of difficulty. Learners can complete them individually, in pairs or small groups.

❯ **Teacher explanation:** The teacher explains a language point (maybe with the visual aid of presentation slides, such as PowerPoint, or by writing on a board).

❯ **Group problem-solving activity:** Either the whole class or a small group is given a real-life problem to solve, orally or through reading and writing.

❯ **Learner presentation:** Learners research a chosen topic, prepare their speech and present to the rest of the group.

❯ **Teacher asks questions of learners:** The teacher can ask open or closed questions and can address the whole group or target certain learners by name.

❯ **Tests and quizzes:** Wordsquares, crosswords and word bingo are all popular or learners can test each other on pronunciation or spelling.

❯ **Individual writing task:** Chosen by the teacher or the learner.

TASK 7.3

Consider the range of activities above. Which do you think will enable you to differentiate well and which might be less successful in differentiating?

(Adapted from Petty: see further reading, p. 95)

Deep and surface learning

Read this poem:

'Twas brillig, and the slithy toves
Did gyre and gimble in the wabe;
All mimsy were the borogroves,
And the mome raths outgrabe.

Lewis Carroll 'Jabberwocky'

Can you answer these questions?

1. Where did the slithy toves gyre and gimble?

2. What did the mome raths do?

3. Why were the borogroves all mimsy?

4. Why might they be easy or difficult to answer?

You probably found it reasonably easy to answer questions 1 and 2 and impossible to answer question 3. This is because the first two questions rely on understanding only the grammatical structure of the poem. If it is a question enquiring 'where', we expect the answer to be a prepositional phrase (in this case, describing a place). If the question asks what something is doing, then the answer must be a verb. We do not need to understand what we read to answer this question. We can say 'the mome raths outgrabe' because we see it in the poem, but we are repeating what we see without real understanding. However, to answer question 3, you need to understand the text in more depth, and because we cannot read (or create meaning from the text), we cannot answer it.

Questions 1 and 2 could be termed 'surface learning' – they are easy to answer but don't take you very far. For deep learning to occur we need to ask different types of questions. Benjamin Bloom (1964) devised a taxonomy of activities in the cognitive realm which have often been illustrated by a triangle as pictured in Figure 7.1. The taxonomy (or classification) starts with the tasks that are easiest; these get progressively more complex as one moves up the triangle.

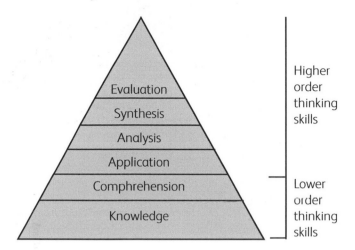

Figure 7.1 Bloom's Taxonomy

Petty (2009) has drawn on Bloom's taxonomy to divide tasks into two types, involving higher and lower order skills and leading to deep or surface learning. He calls them *mastery* and *developmental* tasks. To avoid any confusion, we have renamed them *achievable* and *stretching* tasks.

Achievable tasks

❯ Easy, typically involving only knowledge and comprehension (lower order skills)

❯ Not dependent on prior learning

❯ Can be attained in a short time

❯ All learners should be able to get them right

Stretching tasks

❯ Involve higher order skills like evaluation and synthesis (higher order skills)

❯ Dependent on prior learning

❯ Development is slow and requires effort

❯ Learners will not get them all right

A differentiated session might involve both types of tasks. One might start with one or more achievable tasks (can be attained in a short time) which would build learners' confidence (all learners can get them right) before moving on to simpler stretching tasks (which are dependent on prior learning) and then maybe to more challenging tasks which involve higher order thinking and which require more effort. The extra work involved can be supported by collaboration and scaffolding by the teacher.

TASK 7.4

What sorts of outcomes might involve tasks that are achievable and which involve stretching tasks? Look at these possible outcomes on an employment-related course.

- Follow fire safety instructions
- Recognise and use ten words relating to pay and conditions
- Complete own CV
- Express personal aspirations
- Respond appropriately to job interview questions
- Research a job of personal interest
- Recognise and follow workplace signs and notices
- Fill in a timesheet

When you start teaching, you may have to devise your own scheme of work or you may be given a scheme of work to use that has been written by a more experienced teacher. A scheme of work is never written in stone and needs to be continually reassessed and updated as you get to know the learners, their individual contexts and their needs and interests. So whoever has written it, you will need to look at it carefully and evaluate it on a continual basis.

These are some of the questions you might want to ask when considering if a scheme of work is appropriate for your literacy or ESOL group:

- How well does it cover all the skills and language in the curriculum?
- How well does it embed language and literacy into other subjects the learners might be studying?
- Does it offer appropriate allocations of time?
- Does it give a broad and balanced curriculum?
- Are there recognisable units of work for each subject area (these may be continuous or blocked units of work)?
- What are the learning objectives to be addressed?
- Is there a logical sequence in which the work will be delivered (progression)?
- Are the activities engaging for the learner group?
- Does it relate to the assessment to be undertaken?
- Does it differentiate enough for the different needs and interests in the group?

❭ Does it utilise the resources that are available (or does it require any that are not available)?

❭ What opportunities are there for formative assessment?

❭ What opportunities are there for monitoring and evaluation?

❭ How does it incorporate record keeping?

If you are not able to answer each question in the affirmative, you will need to make some adjustments to the scheme of work.

FURTHER READING

Hughes, N. and Schwab, I. (2010) *Teaching Adult Literacy: Principles and Practice*. Maidenhead: Open University Press.

Paton, A. and Wilkins, M. (2009) *Teaching Adult ESOL: Principles and Practice*. Maidenhead: Open University Press.

Petty, G. (2009) *Teaching Today: A Practical Guide* (4th edn). Cheltenham: Nelson Thornes.

Petty, G. (n.d.) See: http://geoffpetty.com

8 Professionalism and CPD

Anne McKeown

INTRODUCTION

In this final chapter we consider what it means to be a professional language and/or literacy teacher. We will explore some ways in which you may maintain your professional status, and continue to develop as a practitioner through ongoing continuing professional development (CPD).

Whether teaching is a profession, or not, has long been an issue contested by sociologists. Traditional professions such as law or medicine may be described as having a defined body of knowledge, and certain agreed codes of behaviour or practice. The professional lawyer or doctor is seen as having responsibility to the people they serve and exercises autonomy in their judgments. Unlike these traditional professions, teaching does not have an easily identifiable body of knowledge or defined code of practice. For literacy and ESOL teachers, knowledge about language systems is essential. But there is more to teaching than knowing your subject. Think back to your own experience as a learner. Did you have any teachers that you particularly liked or thought were very good? What was it about them that made them good teachers? Make a note of some of the teacher qualities that you found effective.

Now see if you can organise your ideas about effective teaching under these headings:

Knowledge of the subject and how to teach it	Communication skills	Classroom management	Interpersonal skills
Example: She made the subject really come to life for us.	Example: She explained everything in a way that I could understand.	Example: The class was always calm and a good place to learn.	Example: She seemed really interested in helping me to learn.

Teachers employ many approaches, using their professional judgement as to what is likely to be most effective in any given situation or with any particular group of learners. As you discovered in Chapter 2, approaches to teaching change over time, according to whichever theory of language or literacy learning is most popular. You may find yourself applying behaviourist principles when drilling new language patterns with an ESOL group, or taking a discovery-based, problem-solving approach when working on a project such as planning a class outing. You may draw on theories from cognitive psychology on how an individual relates new knowledge to knowledge already acquired when you elicit from learners what they already know about a topic or context, thus helping them to activate schemata. Alternatively you may focus on the social aspect of learning by relating your lessons to your learners' literacy practices. You may also take a different approach with individuals according to what you have already learned about their language and literacy histories, and their ways of learning. As you become more experienced you will probably find yourself employing all of these approaches at some time in your teaching. Whichever approaches you adopt, you will be concerned to get the best outcomes for all of your learners. You will need to draw on your knowledge of language and your knowledge and understanding of language and literacy learning, as well as develop your skills and abilities to create a positive learning environment for your learners.

PROFESSIONAL VALUES AND PRACTICE

A new set of professional standards was published for teachers in the lifelong learning sector in 2014, replacing the 2007 standards. The new standards outline the skills, knowledge and professional values and attributes expected of teachers in the sector. Some examples of these values and how they might translate into practice are shown here.

Professional value	What this might mean in practice
Reflect on what works best in your teaching and learning to meet the diverse needs of learners. (1)	Literacy and ESOL teachers try to find out about their learners' backgrounds, their experiences and their personal goals. They keep these in mind when planning, teaching and evaluating lessons.

Another value relates to equality, diversity and inclusive practice. Think about your own experience as a new teacher of literacy and/or ESOL. What have you done or observed that could promote equality in the classroom, or ensure that all learners are included? Make a note of your ideas.

You might have thought of some of these ideas:

Professional value	What this might mean in practice
Value and promote social and cultural diversity, equality of opportunity and inclusion. (5)	Some ways in which literacy and ESOL teachers put this value into practice could be as follows: • Choose topics which reflect the learners' backgrounds or experience • Give support for individual learning needs • Use example texts and contexts that reflect the diversity of the society in England

TASK 8.1

Try and think of fifteen ways to describe teaching or teachers – for example, knowledgeable or creative. When you have thought of fifteen, have a look at our suggestions – are the two lists similar? Are there any that you would like to have used to describe you?

How teachers are seen may vary according to different perspectives. Government places great value on achievement – whether through learners gaining qualifications or achievement of other targets, and teacher performance is often measured against their learners' success. Learners themselves may place value on other aspects of their learning experience. Which of the qualities on the list may be most valued by…

❱ college managers?

❱ learners?

❱ you?

Many people come into further education teaching because they hold altruistic values such as wanting to

❱ help people

❱ make a difference

❱ challenge inequalities

❱ empower people

In the day-to-day bustle of teaching, these values sometimes get forgotten or at least seem less immediate. It is important, though, for teachers to reflect on the wider context of language and literacy teaching and re-visit their ideas about the purposes of education. Depending on the context in which you are teaching, you may have opportunities to discuss these ideas with your colleagues. Another way of refreshing and re-invigorating your professional values is by professional networking. Two important professional associations for language and literacy teachers in the UK are:

❱ RaPAL – Research and Practice in Adult Literacy (www.rapal.org.uk)

❱ NATECLA – National Association for Teaching English and other Community Languages to Adults (www.natecla.org.uk)

Both these associations hold conferences and events, publish newsletters and journals, and support professional networking. Membership is open to all on payment of a small annual subscription. If you are new to teaching literacy or ESOL, joining RaPAL or NATECLA is a good way to get to know others in the field and keep up to date with developments.

CONTINUING TO DEVELOP AS A TEACHER

All professionals are responsible for continuing to develop their practice. Once you have finished your initial teacher education programme you will need to make sure that you keep up to date with current thinking on language and literacy teaching. There are many ways in which teachers continue to develop their practice, and continuing professional development (CPD) can take many shapes and sizes. The following are some examples of possible CPD activities you could do, ranging from the informal to more formal structured programmes.

CPD activities
Keep a reflective log
Read texts on teaching language and literacy
Read up on language systems and frameworks
Follow latest research on language and literacy, for example by looking at NRDC or NIACE websites
Follow policy developments that have implications for language and literacy teaching, for example through news articles and reports, or official websites
Join an online blog or discussion forum relating to language and literacy teaching
Attend CPD sessions or short courses on specific aspects of teaching language and literacy
Undertake longer CPD programmes, for example on developing beginner literacy with ESOL learners
Undertake a higher-level academic programme of study in a subject related to language and literacy teaching, for example an MA in Language and Literacy

Informal

Formal

You have probably already undertaken some of these activities and have ideas of more that you could do. You could also think about how you prefer to work – whether by yourself or in collaboration with others. Rate the following CPD ideas according to how much you enjoy working in these ways.

CPD activity	Rating 1–10 (1 = least, 10 = most)
Reading by myself	
Reading a text and then discussing with colleagues	
Reflecting on my own practice and keeping a log of my reflections	
Observing others teach, with follow-up discussion	
Taking part in online discussions	
Going to conferences and sharing ideas	

Working collaboratively may be easier to do if you are working in a context where you have access to good resources and colleagues with whom you can discuss ideas. It could be more difficult if you are working in an isolated context. However, whatever your work context it will be your responsibility to continue to examine your own practice and to identify strengths and areas for development. The best way to do this is through critical reflection.

Reflective practice

You have already read about reflecting on your teaching in Chapter 4. Reflection is very important in helping you to analyse your practice and explore ways in which you can develop. Reflection is important for every aspect of teaching, not just your practical teaching. Here are some extracts from teachers' reflective logs, illustrating issues and events that took place both inside and outside the classroom. Notice how their reflections have helped to shape their future practice.

Read trainee teacher Amy's reflections on behaviour issues in her class:

> I noticed that every time Zara was in my Level 2 class she was very rude and disruptive, shouting out, even swearing sometimes, not taking any notice of me, not doing anything I asked. I was upset and shocked because I felt that she didn't respect me as a teacher and began to wonder why. What could I do to make her respect me? I began to doubt myself and my ability to become a good teacher.
>
> … Last week I was observing my mentor teach the same class and was really surprised to see that Zara behaved in the same way in my mentor's lesson, and my mentor is a really strong teacher.

... I talked with another teacher and he told me that Zara was often rude and badly-behaved in other classes too. This really got me thinking. I'd been so wrapped up in myself that I'd taken Zara's behaviour as a personal offence and reacted emotionally to it, when really it could be that it was not a reflection on me at all, but more about Zara herself and issues she might have. I began to realise that I needed to think more about where my learners are coming from and what issues they might have which affect the way they behave in my lessons. I realised that my emotional reaction wasn't helpful, what I need to do is find out more about my learners' individual needs.

Amy's reflections show her developing as a professional, able to put aside her personal response and beginning to focus more on the development of her learners. It is not always easy to ignore our emotional responses to things that happen in the classroom, but it is important to recognise them and make sure that our decisions and actions are based on a professional rather than personal response.

Read Abby's reflections on being observed by her tutor:

... Well, I was really nervous about my tutor coming to observe me so I decided to try to make the lesson really fun so he could see how the learners enjoy my lessons. I decided to start off with a quiz and then get them to play hangman and then do a spelling test because they always like spelling tests.

... I thought the lesson went well, they all seemed to be enjoying it and joining in. Some of them even got the spellings right.

... I was really disappointed with the feedback I got from my tutor. He said he didn't think they had learned anything and that all I had been doing was testing what they already knew. He also said I should have clear language and literacy objectives and aim to develop skills in a context which the learners find relevant.

...Since then he's given me some suggestions for what sort of objectives I might set for my lessons. I can see now that I need to think more about what my learners are learning and not so much about how to fill the time with fun activities. I'm getting some good comments about my lessons from learners too – Toni said he'd learned a lot of new words this morning, that was great.

Abby shows a developing ability to respond to feedback and use it to develop her planning. Although her first response to the feedback from her tutor was defensive, she later came to see his point of view and tried putting his suggestions into practice. It is often helpful to look back over your earlier reflections and see how your thinking may have changed.

Read Kazim's reflections on receiving negative feedback:

My Level 1 class are really hard work – they don't seem to remember anything from one lesson to the next and they're really bad at doing their homework. I have to keep telling them the same things.

... Last week my mentor observed me giving back some writing they'd done in class ... when I saw her for feedback a couple of days later I was horrified at some of the things she said to me – she said I wasn't speaking to the learners in the right way and a lot of

other things that were quite personal and that made me feel really bad. I went home feeling worse than I had at any time since starting my teaching placement.

... I've thought about her behaviour more since then. She was wrong to say some of those things to me – they weren't helping me to become a better teacher. But then I thought about how it felt to receive negative feedback and that made me think about how my learners must feel when I give them feedback on their writing. I've realised I need to be more encouraging and comment on things they do well, as well as show them what they need to do to improve. Although the experience with my mentor was awful, I've learnt to think more about the impact of my feedback on my learners and to try to be more encouraging and constructive.

These excerpts from Kazim's reflective log show his development as a reflective practitioner. Although he had a bad experience of receiving negative feedback from his mentor, he was able to further reflect on it in relation to his own practice and his way of giving feedback to his learners. It was unfortunate that he had such a difficult time, but he has made a good professional response to a bad situation.

Reflection is very important for developing practice on a day-to-day basis, but it is also important to reflect over a longer period and to use reflection to help plan your future development. In the next section we look at how reflection is necessary for planning your ongoing CPD.

PROFESSIONAL DEVELOPMENT PLANNING

The first step in professional development planning is to look back over your practice and reflect on your strengths and the aspects of your practice that you would like to develop further. You may base your reflections on your own thoughts and ideas, perhaps from your reflective log, and on feedback you may have had from others, your manager, colleagues and learners. When you have identified some areas for development you need to plan how and when you are going to address them.

We've already seen how CPD can mean many different types of activity. To help you plan your CPD, it may be useful to think about some of the different purposes of CPD. Here are some areas for development identified by trainee teachers at the end of their initial teacher education programme:

> ❭ I need to find out more about phonology and how to teach it

> ❭ I'd like to improve my knowledge of grammar

> ❭ I want to find out more about research into using phonic approaches with adults and what it implies for teaching

> ❭ I need to learn how to use the interactive whiteboard more creatively in my teaching

> ❭ I'd like to learn more about teaching Level 2 and GCSE English

> ❭ I need to do some training on invigilating the speaking and listening exams

These trainee teachers' development aims were extremely varied and included aims relating to:

1. Subject knowledge

2. Knowledge of how to teach

3. Classroom skills

4. Processes and procedures

Some of the aims related to a specific aspect of teaching, for example phonology. Some related to more general aims, for example teaching at a different level or a particular type of programme.

At the end of her initial teacher education programme, trainee teacher Elli organised her CPD aims according to these headings: subject knowledge, practical teaching, further reading and research, college processes and procedures. She drew on feedback she had received during the programme to identify her strengths and areas for future development under each heading:

	Strengths	Areas for development
1. Subject knowledge	Good knowledge of verb grammar Good awareness of phonology	I'd like to know more about identifying and describing features of literary texts
2. Practical teaching	Well-planned sessions Attractive resources Lively classroom manner	I need to develop ways of supporting my learners to read critically
3. Further reading and research	I've read quite a lot about task-based approaches	I'm interested in finding out more about how they work in the literacy classroom
4. Processes and procedures	I've attended the health and safety training I've had a little experience of moderating marking of the writing exams	I need more training and practice in moderating my marking of learners' writing

Once she had identified her areas for development, Elli thought about how and when she could address them. She came up with a professional development plan for her CPD for the following year. Here is an extract from her plan:

Area for development for	Action	Timing
Knowledge of identifying and describing literary texts	Ask my line manager to recommend some reading on literary texts and read up on this.	Before the start of the next academic year, July and August
Using task-based approaches in literacy teaching	Sign up for CPD session	Staff development days in January
Training and practice in moderating marking	Attend team moderation training sessions	November and February

She discussed her plan with her line manager, who agreed with her actions and supported her to carry them through. Her line manager also asked her to attend a college-wide CPD session on safeguarding. Elli and her line manager reviewed her progress against her planned action when they met for an appraisal in March the following year. They made a further CPD plan for the coming year.

Many centres have a pro forma for planning CPD. Here is an example template you might find useful for planning and reviewing your CPD.

Individual CPD planning template

Name ....…. Job title ....

Department ....

Line manager .... Date of review ....

Subject knowledge	
Strengths	Areas for development

Practical teaching	
Strengths	Areas for development

Further reading and research	
Strengths	Areas for development

College processes and procedures	
Strengths	Areas for development

Agreed actions	Action by (who)	Action by (when)
1		
2		
3		
4		

Review date ....

Signed (tutor) ....

Signed (line manager) ....……....

FURTHER READING

Education and Training Foundation (2014) *2014 Professional Standards for Teachers and Trainers.* At: http://www.et-foundation.co.uk/wp-content/uploads/2014/05/4991-Prof-standards-A4_4-2.pdf

Key texts

Albery, D. (2012) *The TKT Course: Knowledge About Language*. Cambridge: Cambridge University Press.

Appleby, Y. and Barton, D. (2008) *Responding to People's Lives*. Leicester: NIACE.

Black, P. et al. (2003) *Assessment for Learning: Putting It Into Practice*. Milton Keynes: Open University Press.

Bloom, B. (1964) *Taxonomy of Educational Objectives. Handbook 1: Cognitive Domain*. London: Longman.

Cooke, M. and Simpson, J. (2008) *ESOL: A Critical Guide*. Oxford: Oxford University Press.

Crystal, D. (1988) *Rediscover Grammar*. London: Longman.

Duncan, S. (2012) *Reading Circles, Novels and Adult Reading Development*. London: Continuum.

Education and Training Foundation (2014) *2014 Professional Standards for Teachers and Trainers*. At: http://www.et-foundation.co.uk/wp-content/uploads/2014/05/4991-Prof-standards-A4_4-2.pdf

Fowler, E. and Mace, J. (2005) *Outside the Classroom: Researching Literacy with Adult Learners*. Leicester: NIACE.

Freire, P. (1972) *Pedagogy of the Oppressed*. Harmondsworth: Penguin Books.

Gower, R., Walters, S. and Phillips, D. (1995) *Teaching Practice Handbook*. London: Macmillan.

Hancock, M. (2003) *English Pronunciation in Use*. Cambridge: Cambridge University Press.

Harmer, J, (2007) *How to Teach English: An Introduction to the Practice of English Language Teaching* (2nd edn). London: Longman.

Hughes, N. and Schwab, I. (2010) *Teaching Adult Literacy: Principles and Practice*. Maidenhead: Open University Press.

Knowles, M., Holton, E.F. and Swanson, R.A. (2011) *The Adult Learner: The Definitive Classic in Adult Education and Human Resource Development* (7th edn). London and New York: Routledge.

Kolb, D. (1984) *Experiential Learning: Experiences as the Source of Learning and Development*. New Jersey: Prentice Hall.

Krashen, S. (1985) *The Input Hypothesis: Issues and Implications*. London: Longman.

Lewis, M. (2002) *Implementing the Lexical Approach: Putting Theory into Practice*. Boston, MA: Thomson Heinle.

Maslow, A. (1970) *Motivation and Personality* (2nd edn). New York: Harper and Row.

NRDC (2007) *Developing Adult Teaching and Learning: Practitioner Guides*. Leicester: NIACE.

- Burton, M., *Reading*
- Cooke, M. and Roberts, C., *ESOL*
- Grief, S., *Writing*

Parrott, M. (2010) *Grammar for English Language Teachers*. Cambridge: Cambridge University Press.

Paton, A. and Wilkins, M. (2009) *Teaching Adult ESOL: Principles and Practice*. Maidenhead: Open University Press.

Petty, G. (2009) *Teaching Today: A Practical Guide* (4th edn). Cheltenham: Nelson Thornes.

Scrivener, J. (2011) *Learning Teaching* (3rd edn). Oxford: Macmillan Education.

Skinner, B.F. (1974) *About Behaviourism*. New York: Random House.

Sunderland, H. and Spiegel, M. (2006) *Teaching Basic Literacy to ESOL Learners*. London: LLU+.

Thornbury, S. (1997) *About Language: Tasks for Teachers of English*. Cambridge: Cambridge University Press.

Thornbury, S. (2005) *Beyond the Sentence: Introducing Discourse Analysis*. London: Macmillan.

Thorne, S. (2008) *Mastering Advanced English Language*. London: Palgrave.

Vygotsky, L. and Kozulin, A. (2012) *Thought and Language* (2nd edn). Cambridge, MA: MIT Press.

Suggested answers to tasks

1. THE LEARNERS

TASK 1.1

Kwame was educated in English and has lived and worked in the UK for six years. He has good spoken English. As he has had at least some secondary education in English, it is likely that he also has some literacy skills in English. **A literacy class would probably be most helpful for Kwame.**

Tomas has studied English for five years and although he is not using his English much at the moment, it is likely that he has much passive knowledge of the language. He is well-educated in his home country, Poland. **Tomas would benefit from an ESOL class.**

Regis has had some education in French, a language which shares a script with English, and also a year's schooling in the UK. It is likely that in that year at an English school he learned to speak English, which he also will need for his job, but he will need to develop his ability to use Standard English if he wants to go on to higher-level study. **A literacy class would be best for Regis.**

Amina has had no previous education and she doesn't use English at home or within her community. **Amina needs an ESOL class; or, if her centre provides it, an ESOL/literacy class, where she can work on developing her literacy skills as well as her English language.**

Jack speaks a regional variety of English. **He needs a literacy class to improve his reading and writing.**

Pearl has been using spoken English for forty years so it is only literacy support that she needs. **She is likely to need a literacy class.**

Irfan's education has been in England. He will have fluent spoken English, although he may not feel confident about it. He also might need help with his written work. He may be able to get extra help with his dyslexia. **Irfan would probably be best placed in a literacy class.**

TASK 1.2

Some of these issues might be placed under more than one heading, for example number 6 may also be placed under personal and social factors.

1.	Whether the learner can read and write in their first language	b
2.	What the learner feels about their previous educational experiences	d
3.	Whether the learner uses English outside the classroom	b
4.	Whether the learner has dyslexia or any other learning difficulty	c
5.	How the learner feels she learns best	c

6.	Whether the learner came to this country from a war zone	e (a)
7.	Whether the learner lives alone or with family or friends	a
8.	What language the learner uses to access the Internet	b
9.	What sorts of things the learner does in his leisure time	a
10.	Whether the learner is employed	a
11.	Whether the learner had any education beyond primary level	d
12.	Whether the learner has children	a
13.	What the learner's preferred language is for speaking	b
14.	Whether the learner was bullied at school	e

TASK 1.3

Tomas speaks an Indo-European language (Polish) and also reads and writes that language. Amina speaks a non-Indo-European language (Somali) and does not read and write it.

The challenge for the teacher in having Tomas and Amina in the same class is that Tomas has had extensive experience of education and is likely to have study skills which he can utilise in his learning of English. These might enable him to pick up English quite quickly. Amina, on the other hand, is likely to be learning how to learn at the same time as getting to grips with both the new language and mastering how to read and write in a language that is not her own. In addition, as she also does not use English much outside the classroom, learning the language might be a slower process for her. The teacher will have to think carefully about differentiating classroom activities in order to support both Tomas and Amina.

2. APPROACHES TO LITERACY AND LANGUAGE TEACHING

TASK 2.1

Cognitive view

> ❭ Learners learn best on their own

> ❭ People need lots of repetition to help them learn

> ❭ Education is where the teacher shares what she knows with her learners

> ❭ Materials should be carefully controlled so that the learners are not faced with anything beyond their level

Social view

> ❭ Learners learn best in groups

> ❭ People need to do a variety of activities in different ways to help them learn

❯ Education is where learners follow their own routes to learning

❯ Materials should be those encountered in real life (realia)

TASK 2.2

In this case the order of events is A–C–R:

❯ **A**uthentic use of language while doing the task

❯ **C**larification and focus by the teacher on language used after the task

❯ **R**estricted use of language, organised by the teacher while practising the language learned at the end of the task

TASK 2.3

Structure

❯ The heading is the name of the dish

❯ There is an indication of how many portions the recipe will provide

❯ The ingredients and the amounts needed are listed

❯ There are step-by-step instructions for what to do in chronological order

Layout

❯ There is an image of how the completed dish should look

❯ The ingredients come before the instructions

❯ The headings are in bold or underlined

❯ The instructions are numbered or bulleted

Language

❯ The reader is addressed directly

❯ Imperative verbs are used

❯ Abbreviations are used for weights and measures (tbsp, ml)

❯ Repetitive use of limited range of vocabulary

TASK 2.4

The headline, while appearing a neutral description of the article to follow, has subtly manipulated the reader's views before they even start reading what follows.

❯ CHILDREN's in capitals to emphasise a sarcastic view of the traveller's arguments

❯ 'Human rights' in inverted commas to suggest this was a spurious claim

❭ The use of the adjective **illegal** (the court case is still proceeding)

❭ The use of the pronoun **you** to draw the reader into the argument and to demonstrate how the reader will lose out

❭ The use of the passive verb **ordered**, which obscures the agency of the action (who has done the ordering?)

3. THE TEACHING AND LEARNING CYCLE

TASK 3.1

These are just some of the adjustments you may have suggested. You will find many other ideas incorporated into the Access for All sections of the National Core Curricula:

❭ *ESOL Core Curriculum*: http://www.excellencegateway.org.uk/node/1516

❭ *Adult Literacy Core Curriculum*: http://www.excellencegateway.org.uk/node/1515

Visual impairments

❭ Enlarge print on photocopies or print-outs; increase size of print on screen

❭ Ensure there is plenty of white space on a page and good contrast in the print

❭ Use blue or black pens when writing on the board

Hearing impairments

❭ Make sure you face the learner so he can see your face and your lips

❭ Group work can be difficult for deaf people. If a question comes from the back of the room, repeat it before giving an answer

❭ Unknown vocabulary is hard to lip-read. Write new words on the board

Cognitive disabilities such as dyslexia

❭ Help learners explore what type of learning suits them best and find materials and approaches that fit with this

❭ Ensure that you place new learning within a clear context and allow learners sight of the 'big picture' by using diagrams or mind maps

❭ Discuss with learners if printing on coloured paper or using a coloured screen background might make reading easier for them

Mental illness

❭ Make sure you have a variety of activities and be flexible to respond to variations in ability to concentrate

❭ Provide a supportive environment, plenty of encouragement and reassurance

❭ Allow learners to withdraw from the group if they feel uncomfortable

TASK 3.2

1. Spell my children's names correctly – **specific and measurable**
2. Write an email to a friend – **specific and measurable**
3. Practise my handwriting – **not specific and measurable (what am I aiming at?)**
4. Be more confident – **not specific and measurable (how will I know whether I am more confident?)**
5. Proofread a formal letter for spelling mistakes – **specific and measurable**
6. Speak clearly in class – **not specific and measurable (what does 'clearly' mean?)**
7. Read five signs in college – **specific and measurable**
8. Improve my spelling – **not specific and measurable (how much does it need to improve?)**
9. Use the past simple tense – **not specific and measurable (in speaking or writing? What if I can use it in some cases and not others?)**
10. Pick out main points from a chapter in my sociology text book – **specific and measurable**

TASK 3.3

Teacher factors

❭ The lesson plan

❭ The learning materials

❭ Communication between teacher and learners

❭ Clear aims and objectives

Learner factors

❭ Learners' engagement with the topic

❭ Group dynamics

❭ Communication between learners

Factors relating to the learning context

❱ The layout of the room

❱ Availability of ICT

4. TEACHING PRACTICE

TASK 4.1

1. 'Look at these job advertisements. [Holds up handout so that everyone can see it.] First, read the advertisements and decide what the jobs are. Write your answer next to the advertisement. Then underline all of the adjectives on the page and decide if they describe a job or a person. Carlos, what should you do first? And then? Do you need to write anything? [Checks with someone else.] 'Any questions? You have two minutes.' [Now gives out the handouts.]

2. 'You are going to listen to a recording. How many people are talking and what is the situation?' [Plays recording.] 'Check your answers with your partner.' [Takes feedback.] 'Now, listen again and see if the questions in the recording are the same as those on the board.' [Points to questions on the board.] 'Write down the number of any questions that you hear, check.' [Points to the numbers next to the questions on the board.] 'Tara, are you going to write anything?' [Checks with someone else.] 'Any questions?'

TASK 4.2

The answers below are just suggestions, you should use gestures that you feel comfortable with. As long as you use them consistently (and they are reasonably intuitive to understand), learners will soon get what you mean.

Stop talking/working: You need to ensure that you are standing at the front of the group where everyone can see you clearly – whatever you do is most effective if you move slowly to that position or stand up if you were sitting while they were working. Many teachers use a visual symbol such as a raised hand, others clap once or even ring a bell to signal the end of, or pause in, the activity. The important thing to remember is that it takes time for people to finish a sentence and come to a natural pause in their engagement, so don't expect (or demand) immediate silence. Once learners get used to what you do you will be able to just stand in position and the class will gradually fall silent.

Work in pairs: A simple hand gesture seems to work best here. Extend your hands towards two learners and move them together to indicate who should work with whom. You can then go round the class assigning pairs in the same way.

Listen to you: This is a straightforward one – most teachers just cup their ear to say 'Listen to me'. Remember that you first need to get everyone's attention.

Mark stress in a word: The first thing you need to do here is to elicit the number of syllables in a word, then you can indicate this by holding up the correct number of fingers. You can then point to or hold the finger that represents the stressed syllable. As well as this visual marker it is good to represent stress patterns aurally and kinaesthetically by clapping – giving the stressed syllable a louder clap. So, *chocolate* is represented by *CLAP clap* and beginner by *clap, CLAP, clap.*

The past or future tense: If you want to encourage a learner to self-correct when they have made a mistake with the tense, perhaps using the present form of a verb rather than the past ('Yesterday I go to the cinema') you can just stay silent and point over your shoulder to indicate the past. Use the opposite gesture to suggest that the learner needs to use a future tense.

5. LANGUAGE KNOWLEDGE

TASK 5.1

> **Eccentric**

> **Word class:** adjective

> **Meaning:** odd

> **Connotation:** positive

> **Register:** neutral

> **Pronunciation:** cc is pronounced x and the stress is on the second syllable

> **Collocation:** person, style, behaviour

> **Morphology:** noun 'eccentricity', adverb 'eccentrically'

Patient

> 'Patient' has two meanings: it can be a noun (a person who is receiving some kind of healthcare) or an adjective (to describe someone who is prepared to wait for something).

> It has a neutral register and neutral connotations.

> The first 't' is pronounced as 'sh' and the 'ie' is pronounced with a weak schwa /ə/ (see section on pronunciation) so neither spelling nor pronunciation are straightforward. The stress is always on the first syllable.

> In terms of morphology, the abstract noun form is 'patience', the negative form is 'impatient' and the adverb form is 'patiently'.

> In terms of collocation, we can say, for example, in-patient, dental patient, to have/lack patience, to try someone's patience, to wait patiently.

TASK 5.2

> **Needlessly:** The noun 'need' plus the adjectival suffix 'less' forms an adjective (*needless*) and with the addition of 'ly' becomes an adverb.

> **Systemically:** The noun 'system' plus the adjectival suffix 'ic' forms an adjective (*systematic*) and with the addition of 'ally' becomes an adverb.

> **Disqualified:** The verb 'qualify' plus the adjectival suffix 'ied' forms an adjective (*qualified*)

and is made negative by the prefix 'dis'.

> **Dirtiest:** The noun 'dirt' plus the adjectival suffix 'y' forms an adjective (*dirty*); the 'y' changes to 'i' when the superlative suffix 'est' is added.

> **Illogical:** The noun 'logic' plus the adjectival suffix 'al' forms an adjective (*logical*) and is made negative by the prefix 'dis'.

TASK 5.3

Prefix	Meaning	Examples
re	again	reread (verb)
extra	outside	extraordinary (adj.)
under	not enough	underweight (adj.) underachieve (verb)
over	too much	overeat (verb)
inter	between	international (adj.)
mis	wrongly	misapply (a rule) (verb)
mid	middle	mid-flow (noun)
pre	before	predate (verb)
post	after	postnatal (adj.)
anti	against	anti-war (adj.)

TASK 5.4

a)

> Arrive – arrival

> Employ – employment

> Work – worker

> Bore – boredom

> Child – childhood

> Train – trainee

> Depend – dependence

> Happy – happiness

> Liable – liability

> Attract – attraction

> Invite – invitation

b)

❭ Read – readable

❭ Snow – snowy

❭ Beauty – beautiful

❭ Wire – wireless

❭ Tropic – tropical

❭ Fame – famous

❭ Attract – attractive

TASK 5.5

'A taste of your own medicine': The register is informal; it usually collocates with the verb 'to give someone' or 'to get' and has quite negative and challenging connotations. As such, it could cause offence.

TASK 5.6

❭ '-s' is used for the third person singular in the present simple, for example 'he works'.

❭ '-ed' is used to form the past tense or past participle of regular verbs, for example 'he worked', 'he had worked'.

❭ '-ing' is used in continuous tenses, for example 'he was working', to make a noun from a verb, for example 'swimming is good for you', or to form a present participle, for example 'While waiting, I made some phone calls.'

❭ '-en' is used to form the past participle of some irregular verbs, for example 'we were forgotten'.

TASK 5.7

I had never paid much attention **to** history at school because I was never very good **at** it but when I grew **up** I was interested **in** finding out more about the origins **of** the town where I lived.

TASK 5.8

1. Bill is trying to lose weight. (Problem, challenge)

   He has tried going to the gym more often. (Solution)

2. Steve has stopped smoking at last. (He doesn't do this anymore)

   He stopped to talk to me. (He stopped doing something else and started to talk)

3. Jill remembers sitting on her grandmother's knee as a child. (A memory of the past)

   Please remember to post this on your way home. (Referring to a task that needs doing in the future)

TASK 5.9

	Tense	Time
I would rather you **didn't smoke** in here	Past simple	Present
I wish I **had** more free time	Past simple	Present
I **was wondering** if you could lend me a tenner	Past continuous	Present
The film **starts** at 8.30pm	Present simple	Future

TASK 5.10

1. Likelihood
2. Recommendation
3. Ability
4. Opinion
5. Likelihood

TASK 5.11

and	but	so	or
Furthermore	Nevertheless	Therefore	Otherwise
Moreover	Although	Hence	Alternatively
Also	However		
In addition			

TASK 5.12

1. There is a lexical set around air travel: air passengers, flight, planes, and long haul.

2. Passengers

3. No-child

4. After '35 %', 'of air passengers' is missed out.

5. 'The survey' because 'a survey' has already been mentioned

6. 'would be happy' and 'would be prepared'

TASK 5.13

leave /iː/, part /ɑː/

/raw /ɔː/

TASK 5.14

Here /ɪə/, paid /eɪ/, toy /ɔɪ/, strive /aɪ/, now /aʊ/

TASK 5.15

<u>At</u> ten <u>to</u> two, I left <u>the</u> house <u>to</u> meet <u>a</u> friend <u>at</u> <u>the</u> stat<u>ion</u> <u>but</u> <u>the</u> train <u>was</u> early <u>and</u> my friend <u>had</u> already got <u>a</u> taxi.

6. THE FOUR SKILLS: SPEAKING, LISTENING, READING, WRITING

TASK 6.1

Making a speech at a wedding

You might have noted: being nervous about speaking in front of a large audience; getting the tone right; being amusing but not offending anyone; poking gentle fun at the happy couple, but not giving away any secrets. These issues are all related to the discourse of wedding speeches and this might be an example of a case where your everyday practices might not serve you well. Becoming familiar with the discourse of wedding speeches will make you more comfortable with this new practice.

Writing a condolence letter

You might have written here: knowing what to say and how to put it in a way that gives support to the bereaved person; knowing how to begin and end such a letter; how long and how personal it should be. While you probably don't want to get the spelling and grammar wrong in a letter like this, that is not the biggest hurdle. Instead, it is being able to express your feelings in a way that makes you feel like you've said what you meant to say with the right tone and in the appropriate format.

Reading a legal document

The main problem here is that it is difficult to understand what it says.

There may be issues with *domain-specific vocabulary*. It is very hard to make sense of any text without the requisite vocabulary. Legal texts often make use of technical terminology and archaic, formal or unusual words (such as aforesaid, wheresoever, null and void, plaintiff).

Legal and other official texts tend to use *complex sentence structure* to explain complex ideas and to make sure these cannot be read in alternate ways. They tend to be impersonal and make extensive use of negative and passive constructions. The sentences are longer than those in other types of discourse and when reading a text of this type, it is sometimes hard to use your normal strategies to decipher difficult texts (for example, to find the main clause and trace the subject of the main verb).

A further problem for the reader might be lack of *background knowledge*. If you don't have much prior knowledge of the topic of the text, it will be hard to interpret what it means. Where we can link what we read with our schema of the content (what we already know about it), we will find it much easier to comprehend it and make it mean something.

TASK 6.2

You may have noted:

❯ conventional **language** items such as 'Dear Sir/Madam; I am writing in response to your letter of ... Yours sincerely/faithfully'

❯ **structural** items **such as how to** start and finish the letter when you know or do not know the recipient of the letter; paragraphing (we sometimes think of a formal letter having three main paragraphs: reason for writing; main content; and conclusion)

❯ **layout** issues such as where to put your own and the recipient's address; the date; and how to align the different parts.

TASK 6.3

Email to?	Language	Structure	Layout
1. Your child away at university	Informal	May be quite unstructured without paragraphs	Use of forenames; informal signing off, not necessarily on separate lines
2. Work colleague	Semi-formal	May be formally structured (but not necessarily if it's a quick response)	Probable use of forenames (but may be dependent on your relative levels of seniority); quick sign off
3. The council about council tax	Formal	Clearly structured with each point in a separate paragraph	Formal layout with use of surnames and titles; formal sign off on separate lines

TASK 6.4

Audience order from most familiarity to least familiarity (i.e. least formal to most formal):

a. 4

b. 2

c. 1

d. 3

TASK 6.5

It will depend on the context of the task but here are some possible answers.

	Suitable for literacy, ESOL or both?	Does it practise speaking, listening or both?	What is it useful for?
Discussion	Both	Both	Authentic language use, developing ideas, responding to others' ideas, group cohesion
Role play	Both	Both	Authentic language use, practice of particular functions
Prepared presentation	Both	Speaking for the person giving the presentation, but also listening for the audience	Extended and/or formal speaking, delivering to a live audience
Communication games and tasks	Mainly ESOL	Could be both depending on the task	Depends on task, but can be fun and motivating way of controlled practice
Drilling and controlled practice	ESOL	Mainly speaking	Controlled practice of particular language items and responses

TASK 6.6

	What is the purpose of the listening (what are you listening for)?	What might be difficult about it?	Do you need to speak as well as listen?
Your doctor is giving you the result of some tests	To find out what the tests show	Emotional response getting in the way of hearing key information	Yes, to ask questions
Weather forecast on the radio	To find out what the weather will be like in your area today/ tomorrow	Keeping your concentration until it gets to the point where your details are explained	No
Someone giving you directions	To find the way to somewhere	Remembering a complex set of instructions in the right sequence	Yes, to clarify confusions
Chatting to a neighbour in the street	To interact with a friend	Hearing gossip you may not want to know	Yes, to keep conversation flowing

TASK 6.7

	Listening for gist or detail	What details?
Watching a sitcom on TV	Gist	
A friend telling a joke	Detail	The punchline
An announcement at the station	Detail	The train you are waiting for
The answerphone message when you ring an office	Detail	Time the person will be back
A lecture at college	Mainly gist but some detail	Key points

TASK 6.8

Task	Speaking	Listening	Reading	Writing
Helping a child with her homework	Asking her questions	Listening to her reading	Reading along with the child	Writing out words she can't spell
Talking to the doctor	Explaining your symptoms Asking questions	Listening to the doctor's explanations	Leaflets Prescription	Making notes on what the doctor says
Travelling somewhere new on the bus	Stating your destination and asking for the ticket	The driver/conductor's instructions on where to get off	A map or the destination on the front of the bus	Copying down directions to unfamiliar destinations
Checking your Facebook page	Discussing content with a friend	Discussing content with a friend	Reading latest posts	Responding to posts

7. PLANNING LEARNING FOR INCLUSIVE PRACTICE

TASK 7.1

Some of the factors you might have mentioned are:

❯ Learning theory

❯ Approaches to language and literacy teaching

❯ The relevant core curriculum (literacy or ESOL)

❯ The number of learners taking the course

❯ Learners' needs as identified by initial/diagnostic assessment

❯ Learners' aspirations

❯ Learners' interests

❯ The context in which the learning tales place

❯ Physical factors such as the layout of the room and number of tables

❯ Materials and resources available (for example, sets of course books or an interactive whiteboard)

❯ The time available to run the course

❯ The accreditation/qualification the learners are aiming for

TASK 7.2

You can check your answer by looking at the literacy core curriculum:
http://www.excellencegateway.org.uk/node/1515

❱ Sentence beginning and ending (Ws/E1.1)

❱ Question mark (Ws/E2.3)

❱ Capital letters for proper nouns (Ws/E2.4)

❱ Comma (Ws/E3.3)

❱ Apostrophe (Ws/L2.4)

TASK 7.3

Differentiates well

❱ Individual writing task

❱ Group problem-solving activity

❱ Learner presentation

❱ Graduated worksheets

Does not differentiate so well

❱ Teacher explanation

❱ Teacher asks questions of learners

❱ Tests and quizzes

TASK 7.4

Achievable tasks	Stretching tasks	Might be either
Recognise and follow workplace signs and notices	Complete own CV	Respond appropriately to job interview questions
Fill in a timesheet	Research a job of personal interest	
Follow fire safety instructions	Express personal aspirations	
Recognise and use ten words relating to pay and conditions		

8. PROFESSIONALISM AND CPD

TASK 8.1

》 efficient

》 caring

》 hard-working

》 punctual

》 knowledgeable

》 good at organising

》 well-organised

》 creative

》 reflective

》 fun

》 thoughtful

》 nterested in the learners

》 effective

》 innovative

》 passionate

(There are many other possibilities of course…)

Index